PRAYING
The 23rd Psalm

ELMER L. TOWNS

Regal

A Division of Gospel Light
Ventura, California, U.S.A.

Published by Regal Books
From Gospel Light
Ventura, California, U.S.A.
Printed in the U.S.A.

Regal Books is a ministry of Gospel Light, an evangelical Christian publisher dedi-
cated to serving the local church. We believe God's vision for Gospel Light is to pro-
vide church leaders with biblical, user-friendly materials that will help them evan-
gelize, disciple and minister to children, youth and families.

It is our prayer that this Regal book will help you discover biblical truth for your own
life and help you meet the needs of others. May God richly bless you.

*For a free catalog of resources from Regal Books/Gospel Light, please call your Christian sup-
plier or contact us at 1-800-4-GOSPEL or www.regalbooks.com.*

Cover and Internal Design by Robert Williams
Edited by Kyle Duncan

Library of Congress Cataloging-in-Publication Data
Towns, Elmer L.
    Praying the 23rd Psalm / Elmer L. Towns.
        p.   cm.
    ISBN 0-8307-2776-0
    1. Bible. O.T. Psalms XXIII—Meditations.   I. Title.

BS1450 23rd .T68   2001
242'.5—dc21   2001019317

3   4   5   6   7   8   9   10   11   12   13   14   15   /   09   08   07   06   05   04   03   02

Rights for publishing this book in other languages are contracted by Gospel Light
Worldwide, the international nonprofit ministry of Gospel Light. Gospel Light Worldwide
also provides publishing and technical assistance to international publishers dedicated
to producing Sunday School and Vacation Bible School curricula and books in the lan-
guages of the world. For additional information, visit www.gospellightworldwide.org;
write to Gospel Light Worldwide, P.O. Box 3875, Ventura, CA 93006; or send an e-mail to
info@gospellightworldwide.org.

CONTENTS

PART I

What the Shepherd Does

PART II

What His Sheep Receive

God has used Elmer Towns
to turn a comforting and precious
psalm into a powerful prayer.
Every chapter is filled with fresh,
last-days revelation.

JOHN KILPATRICK
SENIOR PASTOR, BROWNSVILLE ASSEMBLY OF GOD
PENSACOLA, FLORIDA

INTRODUCTION
THE BEST-KNOWN CHAPTER IN THE BIBLE

If you have not already discovered it, I want to introduce you to a growing trend of praying the Scriptures. People are turning specific Bible passages into the prayer of their hearts. Maybe you simply read the Bible, and that's wonderful. But I would like to help you take your Bible reading to a higher level. I began praying the Scriptures a few years ago, and now I invite you to join me. I began by praying my favorite passage in the Bible: the 23rd Psalm.

I memorized the 23rd Psalm as a boy in Sunday School. And each morning my public school class read aloud the 23rd Psalm before we prayed in unison the Lord's Prayer—just as tens of thousands of other school classes used to do. Those are just a couple of the reasons why it is my favorite passage of Scripture.

While there has been no election or contest to determine our society's favorite Bible passage, the 23rd Psalm is clearly one of the most beloved passages of Scripture because of the way it has become woven into the fabric of our lives. We often hear it quoted at funerals, baptisms and other religious services. Many people can quote it verbatim, while many others (inside and outside the Church) who do not know the psalm by heart nevertheless recognize it when they hear it.

Whatever the passage's standing with most of society, the 23rd Psalm is without doubt my favorite.

I know the words, I understand its meaning, and I have preached on it several times. But one day I realized, *I have Psalm 23 in my heart, but I've never prayed from my heart the message of Psalm 23!*

When I began praying this passage, I found the Shepherd made Himself real to me. The Lord came to me as I prayed Psalm 23 and *God touched my life* with the power of its words. As I began daily praying Psalm 23, I found something else happening: *I touched God.*

If that is what you want—to touch God—take a journey with me through Psalm 23. We will travel through this much-traveled psalm by a new way—a path you have never walked—in which you will pray through the 23rd Psalm. As you do, something will happen to you that happened to me: You will touch God. But more importantly, God will touch you.

Elmer L. Towns
From my home at the foot of the Blue Ridge Mountains
Summer 2000

PSALM 23

The LORD is my shepherd;

I shall not want.

He makes me to lie down in green pastures;

He leads me beside the still waters.

He restores my soul;

He leads me in the paths of righteousness

For His name's sake.

Yea, though I walk through the valley of the shadow of death,

I will fear no evil;

For You are with me;

Your rod and Your staff, they comfort me.

You prepare a table before me in the presence of my enemies;

You anoint my head with oil;

My cup runs over.

Surely goodness and mercy shall follow me

All the days of my life;

And I will dwell in the house of the LORD

Forever.

PART I

WHAT THE SHEPHERD DOES

The opening of the 23rd Psalm is the "He" section, which describes the Shepherd's ways of caring for us, His sheep. He does everything for us; we are not required to do anything but follow. He provides and protects when we stay close to Him. Hence, the theme of this portion is *relationship*.

He is my Shepherd and Lord.

He makes me to lie down in green pastures.

He leads me beside still waters.

He restores my soul.

He leads me in paths of righteousness.

Why does the Shepherd do all of these things for His sheep? The Lord does it for His purposes, "for His name's sake" (Psalm 23:3). The Lord has His own reasons for protecting and comforting us. Why? Because that is His nature.

CHAPTER ONE
THE LORD IS MY SHEPHERD

A Sunday School teacher visited a young boy from his class who was dying. *What hope can I give him?* the frustrated teacher thought. He did not know what to say to the boy, because he did not know how to help prepare a young soul to die. Toward the end of the young boy's visit, the teacher said to him, "Remember, the Lord is your Shepherd."

Then, to make it practical so the boy would remember the lesson, the teacher asked the little boy to hold up five fingers. Pointing to each of the boy's fingers, the teacher repeated five words: "The Lord is my Shepherd." Then the teacher asked the boy to repeat the phrase, touching each finger as he said a corresponding word. When the little boy counted to the ring finger—the fourth finger—he grabbed his own chubby finger with his other hand, repeating, "*My* . . . my Shepherd. The Lord is *my* Shepherd."

The next morning the little boy did not wake up. He was asleep in Jesus. The parents found his chubby hand still holding that fourth finger. Truly, in death the Lord was *his* Shepherd.

The LORD is my Shepherd;
I shall not want (Psalm 23:1).

When you say "my Shepherd," you are admitting that you are a sheep—or at least that you act like a sheep and have the needs of a sheep. If you have the characteristics of a sheep, your biggest need is to belong to a shepherd, because sheep cannot make it in the wild without someone to lead them, protect them and care for them.

Lord, I need You.

What kind of shepherd would you choose if the choice were yours to make? Obviously, sheep do not choose their shepherd, but let us just take a couple of minutes to play *What If?* If you were a sheep, what kind of shepherd would you pick?

Before you answer, let me tell you what kind of shepherd most sheep would want to avoid. Your shepherd would not be like a businessman, because he would want to make a profit off of you. Your shepherd would not have the manner of an army sergeant, as he would want to lead you into battle. Your shepherd would not be like a coach, as he would want you to win the big game. And you would not want a king, because he would want to rule you.

You would want none of these! You would want a personal shepherd who loved you, not one who made money off you. You would want a shepherd who would protect you, not one who would get you killed in battle. You would choose a shepherd who knew what you liked to eat and where you liked to go. You would seek someone who knew how to care for you when you were sick. He should know how to protect you from parasites, predators and poison weeds. You would choose a shepherd who would find comfortable places for you to sleep. If you became lost, you would want an unselfish and brave shepherd who would come looking for you.

Lord, I'm glad You first chose me.

Isn't it good to know that you do not have to worry about choosing the right shepherd because *the* Shepherd has chosen you?

When you say "my Shepherd," you are not just telling everyone that the Lord is your personal Shepherd. You are telling the world that you belong to the Shepherd who owns everything. Your Shepherd is really big in this world. He owns it all and created it all—everything. So you never have anything to worry about.

Lord, I want to be Your heir.

Are you wandering in a hot, sweltering desert? He created the burning deserts as well as the cool shaded pastures with crystal clear waters. He knows where everything is located, and He can lead you to relief without looking at a map.

Lord, I need some water.

Are you lost in a dark valley seeing death shadows behind the rocks? You may not know where you are, but He knows. You're not lost to Him; He knows where you are in the valley because He *created* the valley. You can't even get lost in the dark night, because the Lord created darkness, too (see Isaiah 45:7). You may have lost your way, but not the Lord. So take heart; help is coming.

Come quickly, Lord.

After falling into a hole, you may think no one in this world knows your troubles. You are miserable in the hole because you think no one can help you—not your mother . . . not your buddy . . . not your spouse . . . not even a pastor. You are discouraged because the Lord is sitting on a throne up there in heaven and you are mired in a hole. *Wrong!* Your Shepherd is the omnipresent Lord. He may be overseeing heaven, but He is also beside you in the hole. Remember: "Thou art with me" (Psalm 23:4, *KJV*). You have a Shepherd who is present everywhere at the same time, and best of all, the Lord is your Shepherd.

Hello, Lord. I didn't see You standing there.

When the Shepherd brings you home, He does not leave you to graze outside the door. Your Shepherd treats you better than you deserve, better than you expected, because the Lord is good. As your Shepherd, He is good to you. He loves you when you are good, and He loves you when you stray from Him. God is love, and He will always love you.

And Lord, I love You.

You have a wonderful Shepherd. Do you know His name? Because a person's name usually tells something about him or her, you ought to know your Shepherd's name. Why? So you can know Him better.

Your Shepherd's name is *Immanuel*, which means "God with us." He is not just the Lord Most High, exalted in heaven.

> "Behold, the virgin shall be with child, and bear a Son, and they shall call His name Immanuel," which is translated, "God with us" (Matthew 1:23).

Your Shepherd was conceived of a young virgin girl and born in a lowly stable where animals were kept, including sheep not unlike you. His crib was a feeding trough for animals—and sheep like you. He was confined to live in a human body, but He never once sinned. He grew hungry, thirsty and became so tired He fell asleep in the bow of a boat. Some ask, "How would God act if He became a man?" Look at Immanuel, for He is "God with us."

Lord, thank You for coming to show me how You would live in the flesh.

Your Shepherd's name is Redeemer. When you landed in the pawnshop of sin, your Shepherd walked in with the pawn ticket that paid the price for your release. The Bible says you were redeemed "with the precious blood of Christ" (1 Peter 1:19).

Lord, I'm glad Your blood paid the price for my sin.

Your Shepherd's name is Deliverer. Because you disobeyed God's laws, you were destined for punishment. You were heading for hell. What did your Shepherd do? He went after you, and the Bible says He delivered you "from so great a death" (2 Corinthians 1:10).

Lord, I'm glad You delivered me from hell.

Your Shepherd's name is Savior. The Bible says we all have sinned; this includes you (see Romans 3:23). Because the wages of sin is death (see Romans 6:23), you were lost with no hope; but your Savior reached His hand down to save you.

And we have seen and testify that the Father has sent the
Son as Savior of the world (1 John 4:14).

Lord, I'm glad You're still saving people, including me.

How do you describe your Shepherd? Is he tall, skinny, old
or athletic? If you have a shepherd, you ought to know what he
looks like. The appearance of your Shepherd is not described in
the Bible, although we know He came as a baby born in
Bethlehem. He died in the full strength of manhood on a cruel
cross. His physical features are not described because His
appearance is not important, even though He's "chief among
ten thousand" and "altogether lovely" (Song of Songs 5:10,16).
You will learn His description by learning of the things He does
for you.

Your Shepherd is described as "the door" (John 10:7,9) and
"the way" (John 14:6). And although "narrow is the gate and dif-
ficult is the way which leads to life, and there are few who find
it" (Matthew 7:14), He will lead you to heaven.

Lord, show me the way.

Your Shepherd is described as "the light of life" (John 8:12).
This is a dark, scary world when you do not know where you are
going, and there are dangerous pits along the way. When you get
lost in the valley, your Shepherd will light the way.

Lord, shine some light over here on my feet.

Your Shepherd is described as "the resurrection" (John
11:25). One day you will die, but your Shepherd died so you
might live. And when you die, He will raise you up on the last
day.

Lord, I'm counting on You.

Your Shepherd is described as "the bread of life." When you
get hungry along life's path, do not complain. Go looking for
your Shepherd because He said, "He who comes to me shall
never hunger" (John 6:35). Isn't it good to know that your soul
will never be hungry because He will satisfy you? You may miss

a meal or two—some martyrs even starved to death physically—but your Shepherd will give you real soul-satisfaction.

Lord, I want to be satisfied with You.

Your Shepherd is described as "living water" (John 4:10). Do you ever get thirsty? Not thirsty in your throat, but thirsty in your soul? That is soul-thirst. It is when you have taken a drink of cool water, but your heart is still empty . . . your soul is still

Do you need a drink of the Shepherd's water to soothe your parched soul?

scared . . . you still do not know what to do. Your Shepherd said, "Whoever drinks of the water that I shall give him will never thirst" (John 4:14). Are you feeling a little dry? Do you need some of the Shepherd's water to soothe your parched soul?

Lord, I gladly drink from Your cup.

Your Shepherd has a name. It was not given to Him the way your parents gave you a name. Your Shepherd's name came from heaven. An angel visited a young virgin to tell her, "You shall call His name JESUS" (Luke 1:31). Your Shepherd's name is Jesus.

You have a kind Shepherd. When vicious, self-proclaimed executioners wanted to stone to death a woman captured in the act of adultery, Jesus stayed their hands. He told the woman, "Go and sin no more" (John 8:11). Isn't that the sort of kindness you need?

Your Shepherd can take care of sickness. When a woman sneaked up behind Jesus to touch the hem of His garment, she was immediately healed (see Mark 5:27). Do you need a Shepherd who will look after your wounds?

Your Shepherd can get you out of trouble. When a group of mostly experienced fishermen thought they would die at sea in a storm, Jesus came walking to them on the water because they were afraid. Then He calmed the storm and saved them (see Matthew 14:24-27). Wouldn't it be comforting to have someone that strong come to get you out of trouble?

When the multitude was hungry, Jesus fed them with five loaves of bread and two small fish (see Matthew 14:19). Wouldn't it be wonderful to have a Shepherd who makes sure you never go hungry?

What kind of Shepherd do you want? You want one who knows your name. "He calls his own sheep by name" (John 10:3).

You want a Shepherd who knows the future: "And when He brings out His own sheep, He goes before them; and the sheep follow Him, for they know His voice" (John 10:4).

You want a Shepherd who lets you pursue life, liberty and happiness of the soul.

Your Shepherd is Almighty God, your protection and guide.

But your Shepherd also made the most incredible sacrifice in history. He was sinless, but He gave His life for sinful people like you and me. He did not like the idea of dying any more than you do. He prayed, "O my Father, if it is possible, let this cup pass from Me; nevertheless, not as I will, but as You will" (Matthew 26:39).

Then He allowed soldiers to slap Him, beat Him with a leather whip and crown Him with needle-sharp thorns. They finally nailed His hands and feet to a cross and lifted Him up for all to see, and a mob ridiculed Him. His strength was drained as He hung six hours in the blistering sun.

Even then they did not kill Him. Jesus said, "It is finished!" (John 19:30). And bowing his head, He gave up His spirit and His life. Your Shepherd voluntarily gave up His life for you. He said, "I lay down my life that I may take it again. No one takes it from Me" (John 10:17,18).

I need an unselfish Shepherd like You.

Your Shepherd was not conquered by death. They carried His dead body to the grave, but He walked out alive three days later. Now He can give you victory over death and despair. When you face death's valley, He will walk with you through death's door and out the other side because He has already been there. Don't you love Him?

Lord, I do!

Your Turn to Pray

Lord, I live in my little world, looking after my family, my business, my reputation and my friends. Thank You for helping me do these things.

Lord, You are all-powerful . . . all-knowing . . . and everywhere present. Yet You condescended to be concerned about my little world. You care about my insignificant troubles. I praise You for Your love and kindness.

Lord, You are the great God of the universe. Your holy name is pure and Your majesty is awesome. Yet You are kind and gentle to me. Even thought I don't understand why, I humbly accept Your love.

Some people say, "The Lord is *a* shepherd," suggesting that they only know Him as one shepherd among many. But you cannot have many shepherds. There can only be one Shepherd and one path to heaven. Jesus said, "I am the way . . . no one comes to the Father except through Me" (John 14:6). There are not many roads to heaven, there are not many ways to God, and there are not many shepherds. The Lord is the *only* Shepherd.

Can *you* say, "The Lord is *my* Shepherd"?

You should not even say, "The Lord is *the* Shepherd," suggesting by the article "the" that the Lord is the unique Shepherd. While there is some truth that the Lord is *the* Shepherd, it misses the idea of *intimacy*. The Lord really wants more than to be identified as the great God—He wants a personal relationship with you. He wants you to say, "The Lord is *my* Shepherd." Why does He want you to say that? Because that is what He is.

Lord, I thank You for being my Shepherd long before I recognized it.

And don't say, "The Lord is *our* Shepherd," even though that is a true statement. In church we pray, "Our Father who art in heaven," using the plural pronoun to show that we are one among many who come to Him in prayer. But when you pray Psalm 23, you are not one in a crowd; you are not even one in a church congregation. You are the only one who matters, because you belong to the Shepherd and the Shepherd belongs to you. When you relate personally to the Lord, nothing else matters.

Lord, You are mine.

Why must you have a personal shepherd? Why must the Shepherd give you personal attention? Because serpents slithering through the grass will poison sheep, wolves watching in nearby caves will attack sheep, rushing water will drown sheep and high places will cause sheep to fall to their death. And sheep walk through dark, threatening valleys where shadows stalk them. You need a Shepherd; so remember, *the Lord is your shepherd and protector*. He is not just any type of shepherd; He is *your* personal Shepherd who cares for you and will protect you.

Some people think the Lord is their Shepherd *if* they do not sin, but that is not what Psalm 23 says. Other people think the Lord is their Shepherd *if* they read the Bible, pray and give money to the Church. Again, Psalm 23 does not say that. No matter where the sheep stray they belong to the Lord, and the Shepherd will go seeking His sheep. We have never read of the Shepherd kicking a single sheep out from under His care, nor have we ever read where the Shepherd refused to go look for a stray sheep. Why? Because the sheep belong to Him.

Lord, You are my Protector and I belong to You.

Picture a sheep in a meadow. This helpless animal does not worry about where its food is for next week, tomorrow or even the next few minutes. Sheep rely on the shepherd for good grass and green pasture. Sheep do not worry about predators lurking behind rocks, because it is the shepherd's job to worry about protection. Sheep do not have to worry about the coiled snakes, deep water or high places.

Thank You, Lord, for protecting me.

Do you have problems? The question is not how you are going to solve them. If you have problems, the question is *relationship*. Do you know the Lord? Are you His sheep? Stop grazing with your head buried in the grass. Lift your head and look around. Do you see your Shepherd? If so, don't worry. It is His job to protect you. If you are His sheep, the problems belong to the Lord because of His promise: "The Lord is my Shepherd."

Thank You, Lord, for Your constant care.

Some people live in a way that seems to say, "The Lord *used to be* my Shepherd." There are a lot of people who used to go to church, who used to be Sunday School teachers, who used to be faithful. But something happened. When they experienced financial reversals, they turned their back on God. Or they became sick and cursed God because of the pain. Whatever happened, they *used to follow* the Shepherd. But the problem of the past-tense verb is with the sheep, not with the Shepherd. People stray away from the Shepherd, but the Shepherd does not leave the sheep. Remember, the Lord is your *nearby* Shepherd.

Some people say, "The Lord *will be* my Shepherd someday." Are you living in the future? Do you plan to get right with the Lord sometime in the future? Right now you are busy . . . you are having fun . . . you are starting a new job . . . you are pursuing an education. Your life is too hectic for you to say "The Lord is my Shepherd," because you would have to make many changes. But you love the Lord and you know that someday you will need Him, so you say, "The Lord *will be* my Shepherd." Do not describe your relationship with the Lord using a future-tense verb.

Lord, I need You now.

You can have a close relationship with the Lord today. His favorite time is *now*. You can touch the Lord . . . right here . . . right now . . . immediately!

Thank You, God, for not being too busy for me.

Your Turn to Pray

Lord, I have many problems. Some problems are like little stones in my shoe that are irritating and sometimes painful. Other problems are like huge boulders that I try to pretend are not there. I yield my problems to You. Solve them for me. Lord, You know what problems I will face tomorrow and next week. You know the coming storms that I don't even know about. Prepare me for them. I yield my future to You. Lord, help me not to live in the past tense, always remembering what You did for me in the past. Do it again now. Lord, I sometimes live in the future, always planning to do more for You when I get around to it. I will live for You today.

If the Lord is not your Shepherd, then who is? Who shepherds you? If anyone or anything else is your shepherd, you will probably never find the satisfaction you seek in life. That does not mean you won't have fun at worldly gatherings. Nor does it mean you won't experience the thrill of an accomplishment at work or pleasure when your child is born. But if the Lord is not your Shepherd, you will always want something else . . . something more . . . something bigger, better, faster or more expensive.

If the Lord is not your Shepherd, when you get a promotion at work, you will not be happy until you get another one . . . and another. When in sports you play the perfect game, you will not be happy until you do it again. When you make your first million, you will not be happy until you earn your second . . . and third . . . and fourth. No matter what you do in this life, success begets a desire for more success, and you will never be satisfied. But when the Lord is your Shepherd, you will be able to honestly say in your soul, *I shall not want.*

If your *boss* is your shepherd, then you will probably be restless or feverish with life's usual frustrations. As a matter of fact, your boss is placed over you to get the most out of you; his job is to make you do your job. Your boss will never make you feel at rest or make you say, "I shall not want." When your boss feels you no longer want to improve, contribute or be a team player, he will fire you. When you make the Lord your Shepherd, you can honestly confess, "I shall not want."

Is *education* your shepherd? Then you will be constantly disillusioned. The pursuit of truth is a wonderful endeavor; you may become wise and confident. But when you gain truth, as salt on your tongue it makes you even more thirsty. Until you know Jesus, who is the truth, you will not really become happy with what you know or satisfied with who you are. But when the Lord is your Shepherd, you can testify, "I shall not want."

What about enjoyment of life? Is *fun* your shepherd? If you make fun your shepherd, your life will be put on hold. Like an unresponsive telephone, you will never get through. It's important to remember that fun is like the bubble you seek to hold in your hand: The moment you clutch it, it is gone. You can go to the circus to have fun. For weeks you look forward to the circus coming to town, and you anticipate an exciting time. You may laugh and be thrilled with the animals under the big top. When you are there, you have fun. But what happens after you leave and go home? There is an emptiness in your heart. You must repeatedly go back to the circus for more fun. Surely you have your memories; but do you want to spend your life looking at scrapbooks, remembering the fun times you used to have? It is no fun living in the past.

When you know the Shepherd, He gives you enjoyment that is greater than fun. He gives you satisfaction and contentment.

Jesus calls it peace: "Peace I leave with you, My peace I give to you; not as the world gives do I give to you" (John 14:27). You can have an experience that is greater than fun—a trusting relationship with your Shepherd. When you rest securely at His feet, you do not need anything, you do not lack anything and you do not fear anything. Life is peaceful at His feet. You can say, "I shall not want today." As long as you make the Lord your Shepherd, you will always know peace and contentment.

Lord, it's so peaceful lying at Your feet, I never want to leave.

Your Turn to Pray

Lord, I am tired of looking for fun everywhere. I am tired of dead-end streets. I'm tired of running on empty. Be my Shepherd so I shall not want any longer.
Lord, I want to be happy. I want to be at peace with myself.
I want to feel great. May I sit close to You?
Lord, I want to please You and have fellowship with You.
Thank You for taking care of me and protecting me.
Lord, it is so good to feel good, and I feel good when I'm close to You. Help me stay here, and keep me
from straying.

CHAPTER TWO
I SHALL NOT WANT

A well-known minister stood before a Sunday School gathering of small children and asked, "How many of you can quote Psalm 23?" Several of the children raised their hands, among them a beautiful little blonde-headed girl who could not have been much more than four years old. The pastor was surprised that such a young person would know Psalm 23. So he asked her to come to the front of the room to recite it for the class.

Standing before the class with hands clutched behind her back, the young girl smiled, and the minister smiled back. Then, with great confidence, she said only this: "The Lord is my shepherd. That's all I want."

The little girl had the words mixed up, but she got the message right.

The most important thing to understand about Psalm 23 is our relationship to the Shepherd. When we get Him, everything else is secondary. Psalm 23 is less about *where* we go—e.g., beside still waters or through the valley of the shadow of death—than it is about with *whom* we go in a deepening relationship of intimacy. Without the presence of our Good Shepherd, what do we have? Nothing. Everything in this psalm is about our relationship to the Shepherd and His relationship to us.

Lord, can I stand close to You?

The little girl was right. If you take the Shepherd out of the psalm, there is no promise of anything. Why? Because Psalm 23 is about the Shepherd, the person of the Lord Jesus Christ. To get all the blessings of this psalm, you must become preoccupied with Jesus Christ—you must relate to Him.

Lord, be my Shepherd so I can be Your sheep.

When the Shepherd comes into your life, He can take away all "want." "Wow!" you might say. "Then why doesn't everyone get right with the Shepherd? They can be rich and famous, have security—get anything." No, it doesn't work that way. Getting rid of your wants does not begin with filling your wish list. You do not begin with your wants but instead with the Shepherd. You must love the Shepherd, seeking fellowship with Him and asking for His influence in your life. Before you try to get satisfaction *from* the Shepherd, you must get close *to* the Shepherd.

If you look around now, can you see your Shepherd from here?

When the Shepherd gives you eternal life, He has given you everything because He has given you His life. Now you are His sheep, so you belong to Him. He is not going to let you starve; the Shepherd will feed you. The secret is found in *relationship;* to have the benefits of Psalm 23 you must be related to the Shepherd. Remember, you cannot enjoy the *blessings* of the Shepherd if you have not received His offer of *salvation.*

Lord, thank You for being my Savior.

Once you admit "The Lord is my Shepherd," everything else changes. Psalm 23 becomes personal for you. Jesus reminded us of the personal relationship between shepherd and sheep when He said, "He calls his own sheep by name" (John 10:3). Does He know your name?

"The sheep follow him, for they know his voice" (John 10:4). How close must sheep be to their Shepherd? They must be close enough to hear His voice. Are you close enough to hear His voice?

Lord, keep me close enough to hear what You say.

Notice how the first sentence in Psalm 23 is incomplete: "The LORD is my Shepherd; I shall not want." Ask yourself the question, *Want what?* David left the sentence incomplete so you could fill in the blank. *I shall not want money . . . security . . . fame . . .*

things . . . retirement . . . vacation. What is your greatest *want* today? Take a flashlight and search deep within the dark caverns of your heart. What you cherish most is what you complain about most when you lose it. What would cause you to fuss the loudest today? What if you lost your job? Your car? A friend? Your health? What if you were to face death because of terminal cancer? What you stew about the most is what you treasure the most.

Remember when you went to the carnival as a kid and were worried about losing your money? You placed it in your deepest pocket, but you were afraid of losing it on the rides that turned upside down. So you gave it to your father to keep for you. Now take the most precious thing in your life today and give it to your Shepherd for safekeeping. Let your Shepherd worry about those things. Then you can say, "I shall not want."

Lord, keep my money safe for me.

It is hard for you to say, "I shall not want," because you *really want things*! You want to keep them, and you are afraid to give them to the Shepherd because you think He might not give them back. But things break, and eventually you will need a new car because it will wear out. You may need a new house because the present one can fall down. You will need new clothes. What things do you possess that are more important than your relationship with the Shepherd?

Perhaps the problem is not that you possess these things but rather that these things possess *you.* Notice how subtly *things* become *possessions.* At first we possess them, but in the end they possess us. If you stacked all of your possessions in a huge pile in your front yard, poured gasoline on them and burned them up, *then* could you say, "I shall not want"?

Before you light the match, wait a minute. Possessions are not wrong; neither does the Shepherd necessarily want you to live like a hermit. It is all right to have a car. You do have to get to work. And everyone needs a roof over his or her head. You would look funny without clothes, not to mention that you might freeze to death in cold weather. You do need certain things, and the Shepherd knows this. Let Him provide all the things that you need. And when you realize that He provides good things for you to use, you can say, "I shall not want."

It is all right to have things. But know why you have them, who gave them to you and how to use them properly. Make sure that your stuff is always secondary, and be sure that your possessions never possess your heart. Let the Shepherd own your heart and fill your life. When you become preoccupied with Jesus Christ, your Shepherd, then things become secondary—they are only means to an end.

Lord, I yield my things to You.

Sometimes legitimate things lose their legitimacy in your life. Perhaps you have been feeding in a pasture of deep green grass, so when the Shepherd comes to move you away, you refuse to follow Him. You think you know best what to eat, how much to eat and where to eat. As the Shepherd continually calls, you do not answer. The Shepherd leads you away, but you do not follow. Then a legitimate pasture becomes illegitimate to you.

When you will not follow your Shepherd, you are saying that you know more than He does. You are saying you know what is best for your life. But the Shepherd knows when there are dangerous serpents waiting in the lush pasture. Perhaps the Shepherd knows that the pasture is a floodplain and He sees a storm coming. To protect you from the flood the Shepherd tries to lead you away, but you will not listen to Him. The grass that you are eating now may indeed be sufficient for a while, but there is a drought ahead. You may be thinking, *I do not have any wants now*, but what about tomorrow? Tomorrow you may find yourself saying, "I have desperate needs!"

You want to be victorious over Satan, but you are not close enough to the Shepherd to let Him protect you. You want to overcome the dangerous threats to your life, but you do not stay near the Shepherd who will make you an overcomer. There is no victorious Christian life when you stray in victory from your Shepherd.

Your Turn to Pray
Lord, I easily wander off. I am too busy eating to follow You.
And I live in my own small world. Come after me when
I stray, and keep me near Your side.
Lord, I am liable to believe what others say, and I have
a hard time discerning the truth. Keep my eyes focused on You,
and keep them open.
Lord, I have no sense of spiritual danger. Several times
I've almost lost everything. Keep me from the attraction of sin.
Help me choose the right thing.

The word "I" seems so carnal when you say, "I shall not want." How can such a spiritual promise begin with such a selfish word? The problem with "I" is that it has so many different meanings.

The vain person makes the word "I" the dominant force of his life. He says with pride, "I shall not want," because he will not allow anything to come between him and his worldly desires.

The person struggling with self-deprecation has a hard time saying, "I shall not want," because he thinks this is boasting.

Some people use the word "I" without thinking anything at all. "I" is their identity—the glue that holds everything together. "I" tells them where they are going.

What do you mean about yourself when *you* say, "I shall not want"?

We all have wants. When you walk through a store, you may *want* an expensive new dress. You may *want* a new power tool that will make your work a little bit easier. You may *want* a brand-new car, even though you know you can't really afford it. Is that what David meant by "want"? Not really. Often when we say "want," we really mean "desire." A desire is often something you can't have or shouldn't have or don't need.

A little boy sees a beautiful red-and-black coral snake, and he wants it because it is pretty. The boy doesn't realize that what he wants could kill him. The alcoholic says, "I want another drink," but anyone who gives him a drink pushes him closer to a spiraling freefall into hell. A traveling businessman wants to spend the night with a prostitute, but giving in to his desire could destroy his family and ruin his life. Many times the phrase "I want" really means "I lust."

Many of us, like children, do not always want what we say we want. The toddler screams for a toy that another child has, but drops it the moment she gets it. Then she screams for something

When the Shepherd is nearby, you can say confidently, "I shall not want."

else that another child has. What does the child mean when she says, "I want"? She really means, "I am dissatisfied."

Sometimes the thing we want is not a toy, a new car or any tangible thing. What we want most is relief from pain. A baby cries because an open safety pin is scratching his leg. His mother doesn't know what is wrong, so she gives the baby a bottle; but he continues to cry. So the concerned mother tries a rattle, then a pacifier, but her baby continues to cry. The mother takes her baby into her arms to rock him, but the baby continues to cry. Sometimes what you want most is relief because you are hurting. Perhaps you have lost a parent to death, or you have broken up with your girlfriend or you have lost a lot of money.

What is your loss? When you are in right relationship with the Shepherd, He becomes more important to you than anything and anybody. You may lose things, but the loss won't affect you as much if you are close to the Shepherd. He is the most important thing in life. Your concerns will virtually disappear because the Shepherd works all things for good for those who love Him (see Romans 8:28). Know that the Shepherd loves you, He will take care of you and He will keep you from all danger.

Sometimes your deepest wants come from being scared. The teenage boy frets about losing his car because he can't imagine what life would be like without one. A teenage girl can't face life without her friends. What happens when fears become wants? They evaporate when you come close to the Shepherd. When you learn that He will protect you, you begin to ask yourself, *Why should I be afraid?* Are you afraid of the "wolf" that threatens to tear you apart? Stay close to the Shepherd because He has a club that will protect you from the wolves of this life. Are you afraid of falling from high places when walking through the dangerous "mountain passes" of this life? Walk close to the Shepherd. When He is nearby, you can say confidently, "I shall not want."

Some Christians are history majors; they always talk about what God did in the past. They sit on their front-porch rockers and tell stories of what God did for them when they were younger. What they are often saying is, "I used to not want." The Bible does more than tell of past histories; it offers us modern-day solutions. I am convinced that God's favorite word is "now." You need to claim, "The Lord is *now* my Shepherd. I shall not want anything *now*." Tear the pages of previous months from your date book. You don't live there anymore. Focus on *now* and say, "I shall not want anything today!"

Some Christians live in the future. Today they are down and defeated, but they plan to have victory tomorrow. Today they are driven to buy everything they don't have. They can't say, "I shall not want," because today they have a grocery list of things they *absolutely must* have. But the future is a different story. They believe that once they purchase everything on their list, they can say tomorrow, "I shall not want." But today is another story. They don't want to be close to the Shepherd today, because they are busy with their own agendas.

Lord, make me want to be close to You all the time.

What do sheep do when they need something? If they are hungry, they scoot close to the shepherd who feeds them. If they are scared, they huddle next to the shepherd who protects them. Where do you huddle when you have needs? When you say "I shall not want," you are describing the Lord's sufficiency to meet your needs. When the Lord is your Shepherd, He will supply the things you need to remain in fellowship with Him.

Notice what God has *not* promised. He has not said you shall never have any physical problems. You live in a finite body. You will get sick, and all of us will die. "I shall not want" does not mean you will never have physical problems. It means that you can be satisfied with the body you have. You can learn like Paul to be happy in whatever state you find yourself (see Philippians 4:11,12). You may get sick, you may hurt and you may pray earnestly for healing, but you don't have to worry if you are near the Shepherd. He is more concerned than you are about your own hurts.

Some days sheep eat from lush meadows and other days from sparse brown grass. Sometimes you will know financial plenty, while at other times you may face bankruptcy. In your flesh you will likely desire money, cars, bigger houses and finer clothes. But if the Lord is your Shepherd, you must accept what He provides and follow where He leads. The Lord may lead you through a time of famine when there is little to eat. But you must say and *believe*, "I shall not want." Why? Because the Lord is your Shepherd who takes care of you.

Your Turn to Pray

Lord, I confess my life is centered on things like houses, money
and possessions. Forgive me for letting things possess me.
Lord, even when I don't have things, my biggest problem is a
lustful heart that always wants more. Teach me
to be satisfied with You.
Lord, I have many possessions, and I thank You for
providing them. Help me to use them for Your glory.
Lord, I realize I could lose all my possessions at any time.
Help me to live for today and trust You for the future.
Lord, I want You to be the most important thing in my life.
I surrender everything I have to You. Help me every day
to say with sincerity, "I shall not want."

CHAPTER THREE

HE MAKES ME TO LIE DOWN IN GREEN PASTURES

I was a summer-camp counselor leading a group of boys, all 12 years old. The hardest task for me was to make them lie down in their bunks for the mandatory nap each afternoon between two and three. This was the hottest hour of the southern Georgia day, with temperatures often reaching above 90 degrees.

No external force could make 12-year-old boys go to sleep in their bunks at two in the afternoon. So I brought extra desserts from the kitchen with which to bribe them to stay in their bunks. I figured 12-year-old boys are always hungry.

Then I used peer pressure, telling them, "We can't go swimming at three if anyone cuts up, sneaks out or causes a commotion. If one guy cuts up for five minutes, we will all have to wait until five minutes after three."

Then I would pass out wholesome comic books and allow them to trade after they finished reading one. I didn't make them stay in their bunks against their will; I just gave them enough perks to make them *want* to do it. In the same way, the Lord doesn't force us to lie down in green pastures; He just gives us perks to do it (e.g., tender grass, cool shade, clean water, the pleasure of His company).

Have you ever wondered why sheep lie down? Usually, we see sheep standing as they graze in the pasture. But in Psalm 23:2, the Shepherd "makes me to lie down in green pastures." Sometimes sheep grow tired, and the shepherd knows when it is best for them to lie down. Some people love to serve the Lord, but they don't know how to rest in the Lord. There comes a time when the Lord must "make" them lie down in green pastures. Even the Lord Jesus said, "Come aside . . . and rest a while" (Mark 6:31). Do you need spiritual rest?

Most sheep lie down because they are sleepy; they don't sleep well standing up. God has programmed humans so they need about eight hours of sleep each day. As much as you fight sleep and eschew rest, there comes a time when the Lord makes you sleep.

Lord, I rest in You.

When I was in college I hated the idea of going to sleep; there was so much I wanted to do for God. Sure, I devoted quiet time to Bible study and prayer, but I felt I was wasting time if I slept. But then one day I realized that sleep was part of God's plan for all people, including me. If you are a good steward of your body, you will sleep when you need rest. And then as a good steward of your time, you will use your waking hours for His glory.

Lord, restore my body with sleep.

When sheep sense danger, they may lie down in tall grass to hide from a predator. When sheep are standing tall, it's easy for a predator to take them down; but nestled among the grass, sheep can hide from danger. Don't display fleshly courage by seeking out danger. Rather, learn when to hide. Sometimes it's all right not to fight, as we are told to flee temptation (see 2 Timothy 2:22).

Have you ever seen a group of men working hard to dig a ditch? Eventually there come a few moments during the job when they can rest. Some will lean on their shovels; some will sit on the ditch bank; a few will even lie down on the grass. Lying down is one thing that is done when we finish work. As a matter of fact, those who don't work are accused of "lying down on the job."

Lord, I look forward to rest when I've finished my work.

Why do sheep lie down? Because they have finished everything they have to do for the day. Now it's time for rest, sleep, food or just to be near the shepherd. When the shepherd is sitting down, it is only natural for sheep to come and lie next to him. Just like humans crave love, so sheep want the affection of the shepherd as they huddle close to him and lie at his feet. Are you resting near your Shepherd?

Lord, I need You.

Your Turn to Pray
Lord, I still have old inclinations about straying.
The world attracts me and my flesh stirs up wrong desires.
Keep me close to You.
Lord, there have been times when I wandered instead
of lying near You. Make me lie near You in fellowship.
Lord, thank You for seeking me when I went astray.
Thank You for forgiving me.
Thank You for keeping me near to You.

When the shepherd leads his sheep to green pastures, he doesn't wander around until he stumbles across a pasture. The shepherd knows where he's going. The Bible says that God always leads us, which involves a choice on our Lord's part (see 2 Corinthians 2:14). The Shepherd knows where all the pastures are located and which one is right for us. Therefore, the Shepherd takes us to the best pasture—at the right time, with the right food—for today.

The Shepherd doesn't take us to a pasture that is best for other sheep. That's because He knows you by name and loves you. He takes you to choice pastures that have everything you could ever want.

Thank You, Lord, for providing for my needs.

The Shepherd doesn't take you to good pastures of the past—places where you used to feed and enjoyed. Past pastures may not be the best for today. The Shepherd daily chooses today's best.

Likewise, the Shepherd doesn't lead you today to next season's pastures. If He took us to tomorrow's pastures and the grass was not yet green, what good would that do?

During summer in the holy land, the lower pastures are burned up by the scorching Palestinian heat. The shepherd leads his sheep to the summer pastures on the heights and in the mountains where cool breezes blow. But in the wintertime, when cold winds and snow kill the grass in the high plains, the shepherd leads his sheep to the grass down in the protected valleys. Timing is important for the shepherd; he must choose when a pasture is best for his flock.

One commentary on the Hebrew text suggests that the phrase "green pastures" refers to places of "tender grass"—that is, new grass. Tender grass has more nutrients for sheep than old grass. But also, tender grass is easier to chew and is easier on the sheep's digestive system. Sheep will choose tender grass long before they will eat old, tough grass. When our Lord chooses food for you, He gives you tender grass because He knows you will enjoy it. He wants you to have a bounty of food that will make you strong and healthy. Isn't He a wonderful Shepherd?

While the shepherd makes the sheep lie to down in green grass, he is not seen picking the grass for the sheep. The sheep must bend down, bite and chew. In the same way, the Lord doesn't give you eternal truth without your involvement. You must *hear* the spoken Word of God and give attention to understanding it. Then, you must *read* the written Word to better understand what God is saying to you. You must study each book, each chapter and each verse of the Bible.

Since God inspired every word in the Bible, every word is important and has some meaning for you. So know His Word, word for word. Memorize its truth and hide it away in your heart to help you grow in Christ. Finally, meditate on God's Word so it can direct your life. Just as the shepherd takes the sheep into the pasture but makes them responsible for eating, so God gives us the Bible. We are responsible for understanding and applying it to our lives.

Lord, I will master Your Word to me.

Your Turn to Pray

Lord, the food You give me in green pastures is wonderful.
Thank You for feeding me.
Lord, I've never gone hungry when I've rested in Your
presence. Thank You for Your faithfulness.
Lord, when I'm in Your presence, there's enough food.
There's good food and nutritious food.
Thank You for providing all I've ever needed.

The shepherd does not lead his sheep over hill and stream just to show them the pasture. He leads them down into the pastures so they can feed and grow in health and strength. So the Lord does not want you to just enjoy Christianity from afar. Rather, you should walk into a church, learn the Word and serve God there. Christianity is not a museum to be admired; rather, it is a restaurant where we feed our souls.

The Shepherd chooses the pasture for you; you choose if you will eat.

Lord, I will eat in Your pastures.

The words "lie down" have the meaning of repeated action. You are to lie down many times, but that does not mean you are to stay down. There is a time to sleep, but you do not stay in bed all day. There is a time to rest in the pasture, but sheep do not spend their lives resting. The Lord will make you lie down and rest today, but He will do it again tomorrow. The Lord will make you lie down and eat tender grass today, but He will repeat the process tomorrow.

Just as you pray in the Lord's Prayer, "Give us this day our daily bread," so each day the Lord provides enough food for that day. And He will do it again tomorrow. He did it for Elijah in the desert (see 1 Kings 17), He did it for the children of Israel in the wilderness (see Exodus 16), He even does it for the birds of the air (see Matthew 6:26). And He will certainly do it for you.

Some people think it would be wonderful if they could go to church one time and learn enough about God so they would never have to attend again. They want a car that never needs gasoline—a perpetual motion machine. But that's not the way the Lord does it. He makes you lie down repeatedly. Why? Because He wants you to enjoy relationship with Him each day. Repeatedly!

He wants fellowship with you daily. He wants you to pray to Him daily. He wants you to study the Word daily. The Lord keeps many people on a short financial leash. Why? Because if they didn't have to trust God daily for money, they might stray far from Him.

He makes me lie down:

1. Repeatedly
2. Continuously
3. Daily

Why does the shepherd have to make the sheep lie down? When sheep get tired, will they not naturally lie down? Why doesn't the shepherd just wait until the sheep get tired or sleepy? If the Shepherd is close enough to make you lie down, then you are close enough to Him for intimate fellowship. He is near. What are you going to do?

Lord, make me lie down in fellowship with You.

Although the Lord makes His sheep lie down, He does not force us to do it. There is no picture in the psalm of the shepherd pushing his sheep to the ground. He is not tipping them over, nor is he pulling their feet out from under them. Just being in a lush green valley where there is food gives the flock a desire to lie down. If the shepherd has led them through a dangerous valley or through a dry, arid desert, then they will want to lie down when they get to green pastures. The shepherd makes them lie down not by force but rather by providing food. Similarly, a mother does not hold her hand over her baby's eyelids to force sleep on him, but instead, she feeds him so he will fall asleep naturally.

Lord, I will lie at Your feet.

Something else to consider: When a sheep is lying down, it can't wander off. So the Shepherd will make you lie down to keep you from straying from Him.

Lord, may I never stray.

When a sheep is lying down, it's not looking around. When a sheep rests, it's not terribly curious, nor will it wander off. When sheep are standing, there is more likelihood of them straying. While standing, a sheep might look around, and it usually goes where it looks. Isn't that like you and me? We look at tempting things long before we go after them.

Lord, keep me looking at You.

But there's another problem with standing sheep: Some have their heads in the grass. They follow their appetites, and they eat what's in front of them. Eventually, they eat themselves away from the shepherd. But sheep that are lying down don't do that.

Lord, I'll feed in the pasture You provide.

After God's people departed from their bondage in Egypt and entered the wilderness, they became disobedient and refused to do what God instructed. God then sent a plague to chastise them (see Exodus 32:35). Only then did they obey willingly. God doesn't make us go where we don't want to go, but He has His own way of making us willing to follow His directions.

Lord, help me to obey You before I get hurt.

The Shepherd says, "Come to Me," but a young man strays. The Shepherd tells the young man of His love, but the young man loves the things of the world. The Shepherd wants the young man to live for Him, but he instead turns to alcohol for pleasure. How does God deal with such a person when he does not respond to God's declarations of love? He usually amplifies the consequences of sin so that the individual is unwilling to stay in his or her sin. So, finally, alcohol destroys the man's life, alienating his friends and corrupting his self-respect. Only then is he willing to follow the Lord.

The Shepherd says, "Come to Me."

Are you straying from your Shepherd? Do you have a problem with alcohol? Are you struggling with a particular sin? Your Shepherd is waiting for you to return to Him. Don't stay in your sin until you get sick of it. Come to the Shepherd now!

When you pray for God to help you give up a sinful habit, remember that a new life starts with repentance. You must change your mind about the habit and then change your actions. Once you do that, God will help you overcome the habit. God will not just take a habit away from you, but rather, He will make you willing to give up the habit.

So how does the shepherd make his sheep to lie down in green pastures? If it's been a long, hot day, he finds cool, soft grass for the sheep to lie down in. If his flock has not had a good meal, he finds green grass for them to eat. If they have been lost, he brings them home to his pastures. Then the shepherd doesn't have to force them to lie down; all he has to do is lead them into green pastures where they will want to lie down.

When the sheep are quietly lying down, then he fellowships with them. He may play his harp, as David did for his sheep, or even sing for them.

He will rejoice over you with gladness, He will quiet you with His love, He will rejoice over you with singing (Zephaniah 3:17).

But when the shepherd's sheep are standing, moving or wandering, they are not listening to him. Are you lying close to your Shepherd? Are you listening to Him?

Lord, I will stay close and listen to You.

Sheep can't lie on their backs like humans. But you and I can lie in green grass and gaze up at fleecy clouds drifting in the sky. We can sleep in the warm sun and feel the lazy breeze on our faces. When you're lying in the meadow and you smell the earth and feel the grass, then you know that life is good. You feel human in the warm sun.

Your Turn to Pray

Lord, You have repeatedly brought me back to Your pastures and fed me there. Thank You for Your faithfulness.

Lord, right now I am feeding in Your pasture, and fellowshipping with You is wonderful. Thank you for meeting all my needs.

Lord, I am enjoying Your presence. Keep me feeding in Your pastures forever.

I will never leave Your side.

CHAPTER FOUR
HE LEADS ME BESIDE THE STILL WATERS

A sixth-grade boy faced the elementary-school Olympics with uncertainty. For the past three years he had won, leading the boys his age. But it wasn't just that the boy was faster than all the other boys his age. No, he received some extra encouragement from his dad who had been a long-distance runner in college. As the boy ran against his opponents, his father ran ahead of him, yelling encouragement. "You can do it. Come on! Watch the finish line." When distractions caused the boy to look around, the father clapped loudly and pointed to the finish line.

But today was different. The boy felt squeamish when he woke up; he wasn't sick, he just had an uneasy stomach. The boy was afraid he would lose for the first time.

"Don't worry," his father said, "I'll run ahead of you like always." When the starter's gun sounded, the boy dashed out to the lead, but he kept looking around at his opposition. His father ran fast, but the boy didn't keep up. He was busy watching the other boys. The father yelled, clapped his hands and whistled, but still the boy could only manage to come in third place. The father had tried to lead his son, but the father couldn't win the race alone. When the boy took his eyes off his father, he lost the race.

When the Shepherd leads you, that means He goes first. Why? If there is danger lurking nearby, He will face it first. Sometimes there are snakes hidden near the water's edge. If you follow the Shepherd to the cool pond of water, He will deal with the serpents first. You will not know where the serpents are lurking, but He knows, because He knows all things. He can deal with them.

Thank You, Lord, for anticipating danger for me.

There is another reason why the Shepherd leads the way: You don't always know what is good for you, nor do you know the way. The Lord knows the way to the good water, so follow Him. There is an old song about the Lord knowing the way through the wilderness. The chorus reminds us that all you have to do is follow Him.

Sheep have no sense of direction. They can't find their own way, and they need a guide to lead them to water. You are like that. You have no sense of spiritual direction on your own. Yes, you may realize when you are lost, and you know when God is far off, but you will never find Him on your own. God has given you a *conscience* to tell you when you are in danger, and He gives you *correction* to scare you and unsettle you when danger is nearby. You are lost, you are miserable and you ask, *What now?* That's when the Shepherd comes to you and leads you to green pastures and cool, still waters. Will you follow? Or will you stand there in the wilderness, confused and scared?

Lord, thank You for coming to me when I didn't know what to do.

Some sheep are just too rebellious to find water. They don't fight God, butt God or try to bite Him. They are just selfish . . . hardheaded . . . stubborn. They are determined to do what they want to do, when they want to do it, the way they want to do it. You are probably like that sometimes. You have an idea of where there is better water. The Shepherd can't tell you where to find water, and you won't go there by yourself. But He will lead you there. You will follow your Shepherd when He takes you by the hand to walk with you to a cool, still pond of water.

Lord, gently lead me by Your forceful hand.

Your Turn to Pray
*Lord, when I'm lost in the wilderness, when the valley
is dark and when trouble overwhelms me,
let me feel Your presence.*

Lord, when I don't know which way to turn,
when I'm confused and I can't find my way, guide me
to green pastures and cool water.
Lord, there are dangers in my future; some I know about,
others I have yet to encounter. Lead me safely to pastures and
water, and protect me from the evil one.

Suppose the Shepherd *didn't* lead you to water. Only a cruel shepherd would say, "Let them choke in their thirst." No, the shepherd leads his sheep to water because the very nature of the shepherd is to care for his sheep. The Lord loves you, and if you follow Him, He will lead you to satisfying water.

The Shepherd does not stand near the water and call for you to come and drink. Most sheep would never find water if their shepherd did not lead them to it. If a shepherd remained in the wilderness, using his staff to point in the general direction of the water, the sheep would not find it. The shepherd must guide his sheep toward the water, making sure the sheep are with him and are following him. Sheep will follow their shepherd when he guides them.

Lord, make sure I follow You.

Where is the Lord leading you? A shepherd does not lead his sheep into the deep water, for they might drown if they venture in over their heads. He does not lead them into a rushing stream, for they might be swept away by the swift current. He leads them beside still waters. It is in a pool of still water that sheep can drink until their hearts are satisfied.

Lord, there is a pool of still water somewhere. Lead me to it.

Once the sheep arrive at the pool, the shepherd doesn't scoop water into his hands for each sheep, nor does he use a cup from which they can drink. They may need water but do not yet realize it; they may not be ready to drink. You can lead the proverbial horse to water but you can't make him drink; neither can you make sheep drink. All you can do is lead them to a place where they can satisfy their thirst.

And how does the shepherd lead his sheep? Slowly. When a shepherd leads his flock, some sheep are too young to keep up, so the shepherd walks slowly. Other sheep have been injured and are too lame to move fast. The shepherd walks before them, but he does not outdistance them. Why does the shepherd lead his sheep slowly? So they can see him and be near him. The shepherd wants his sheep close by for fellowship because he loves them. He doesn't want to lose a single one. But he also wants them close for protection. When a small lamb falls too far behind the flock, a wolf can easily snatch it. A crippled lamb cannot run away from danger, so the shepherd keeps it close by for protection.

Lord, keep me close to You so I don't get hurt anymore.

Sheep that stay close to the shepherd reach the water first. Those closest to the shepherd also get to the best pastures first. They get the tenderest grass and the coolest water. But most of all, they get to enjoy it with the shepherd by their side. He has led them there. So if you stay close to your Shepherd, He will make sure you are fed daily, that you have enough to eat and that you have the best. Have you been hungry lately? Perhaps you are hungry because you are too far away from the Shepherd.

Lord, I like eating and drinking by Your side.

How will you plan this day? Will you stagger into unknown problems and then deal with them as they rear up in front of you? Or will you walk close to the Shepherd so he can deal with your problems first?

Lord, lead me today.

Your Turn to Pray
*Lord, I'm hungry and thirsty. I need some heavenly food and
everlasting water. Lead me to green pastures and cool water.
Lord, walk slowly so I can keep up. I'm only a spiritual child,
and sometimes I have difficulty following You.*

Lord, I want to walk as close to You as possible.
I need strength that comes from fellowship. I need all the
encouragement I can get.

Isn't it wonderful that the Lord leads us beside still waters but not *into* the waters? The Lord led Moses into the Red Sea because Pharaoh's army was chasing His people. Perhaps you don't know about the danger you will encounter today. All you have to do is walk with the Lord. He wants to lead you beside still waters so He can refresh your soul.

It is also comforting to know that the Lord doesn't lead you to walk on the water. Through the mist the disciples had seen a man walking across the water. They cried out, thinking it was a ghost. When they realized it was Jesus walking on the water,

The Shepherd leads you to where you can rest and recharge your batteries.

Peter cried out in panic, "Lord, if it is You, command me to come to You." The Lord said, "Come." Peter stepped out of the boat and walked on the water toward Jesus. But when he took his eyes off Jesus to look at the storm, he sank (see Matthew 14:28-31).

Walking on water is supernatural. The Shepherd is not asking you to walk on water. He is asking you to follow Him. He will lead you beside still water. You don't have to walk on the water; just drink it.

What do you need to learn from your Shepherd? You may need to learn to trust Him. If your Shepherd leads you into a storm or into the barren desert, He will also lead you out. Eventually, He will lead you to still waters.

Lord, I've had plenty of storms. I need still waters.

Notice that the Shepherd doesn't lead you beside the ocean. You go to the seaside to run in the sand, get a suntan or play in the water. Fun is not what you need from the Shepherd today. You don't need the Good Shepherd to find you a playground. What you need is for the Shepherd to lead you beside still waters so you can rest and recharge your batteries.

Lord, I need renewal.

Notice that the psalm doesn't say the Shepherd leads you to a waterfall. When you sit next to a waterfall, you can enjoy the rushing water, the power, the mighty noise and the movement. A waterfall reminds us that God is the powerful Creator, and there are times when we *need* to remember that He is Almighty God. As the water rushes over the waterfall in its hurried pace to get somewhere else, it reminds us of our tumultous life, flowing toward an unknown tomorrow. There are times when we need to remember that life is rushing by and that we need to make the best use of our time. But not today. This day we need to rest beside still waters where our souls may be restored.

Lord, if I can rest today, I'll work hard tomorrow.

Also, the Shepherd doesn't lead us beside a lake. True, a lake may be still. But when we think of a lake, other thoughts come to mind. We think of a beautiful sunset over the face of the deep water, wildlife in its marshes and even the soft lapping of water upon a sandy beach. When we sit beside a lake, we can meditate on God who is the Creator of it all. But today you need comfort and refreshment. You need the Lord to lead you beside still water so you can drink. You need your soul restored.

Lord, I need rest.

The Lord will lead you to walk *beside* the water, but eventually you will be led to walk *away* from still water. Today has many obligations. You are only walking by these still waters as you journey through this day. When you sit in a hectic conference, look inside for still waters. That pause will give you strength to go on. When the children are fighting or you get caught in traffic gridlock, remember your time beside the still waters. Life has to go on. We need to show up. So let the Lord lead you beside still waters.

Lord, lead me to still waters. Then lead me as I work today.

Your Turn to Pray
Lord, thank You for storms that make me trust in You.
But today I need rest to restore my soul. Feed me and
give me water to drink.
Lord, thank You for powerful waterfalls that teach me Your
omnipotence and for lakes and streams where I can meditate.
But today I need to briefly restore my soul before I meet the
challenges of this day.
Lord, I'll only be here a few moments, so give me
more rest than I can get anyplace else. And help me
make it through the day.

When the Shepherd leads you by a dancing stream, you watch the water bounce over the stones. It spills from one little puddle to another. What you hear is not just the quiet splashing of water upon itself. You hear nature rejoicing—the laughter of our Creator rejoicing in the goodness of water. And when you hear water laughing, you realize it will eventually quiet itself in a still pond, because water always comes to rest—still and quiet in a pond where sheep can drink without anxiety. As you drink there, appreciate the spiritual nature of spiritual water.

Lord, just one taste makes me realize I was more thirsty than I thought.

You know in your heart that still water will refresh and restore your soul and make you new again. You are hot and tired from life's journey. But one drink makes the long walk worthwhile. And the next time you are hot and thirsty you won't mind so much the long distance and the dangerous trail, because you know you are heading home to lie in peaceful green pastures near the Shepherd and to drink from still ponds. My soul is restored because I'm home.

Lord, this is good water.

CHAPTER FIVE

HE RESTORES MY SOUL

David knew the spot well. It was a quiet pool of water that was constantly filled by the small stream flowing in Wadi Kelt. The young teen liked the pool best, even though it was a long walk from his home. Because of the Artesian springs, the pool always had pure water that bubbled out of the heart of the earth. The pool kept the surrounding trees alive in the hottest summers with its life-giving water. When the other pools dried up and the hot breezes killed the surrounding vegetation, David knew he would find food and water for his sheep in the Wadi Kelt.

David slowly led his sheep over the scorched fields. He didn't walk so fast that he would outdistance the young, nor did he wish to push his older sheep too hard in the blistering sun. David heard his sheep bellowing for a drink, but he didn't stop. The wise, young shepherd knew they would soon find relief.

Then David's young eyes spotted the green trees gently being pushed by the hot afternoon wind. When the older sheep picked up the scent of water, their pace quickened. When they arrived, some sheep went straight for the waters. Others began gnawing at the tender grass. Before long, all the sheep were surrounding David, lying in the grass, doing what the young shepherd wanted. David wanted them to eat, drink and rest. There would be no more hot travel today. Now it was time for relaxation and sleep.

The smell of the cool, black earth filled David's nostrils. He felt the soft grass as he laid among his sheep. The aroma of tender grass was perfume to the young shepherd. Just as David led his sheep to a special place for rest and restoration of spirit, so our Shepherd leads us to special places to rest our bodies and revive our hearts.

Have you ever been lost? Have you ever been so disorient-ed that you didn't know where you were going? No one ever intends to get lost. You've never said, "I plan to get lost going to the store." No! You unintentionally get lost. It just hap-pens. Your landmarks are moved or your directions are faulty. Sheep are like that, they never intend to stray. They follow the next bite of grass . . . and the next . . . and eventually they're lost.

The shepherd always takes the initiative to go after his sheep. He will search, call for them and look in every conceiv-able place until he finds his lost ones. When the lost sheep are found, what happens? Does the shepherd punish the sheep for getting lost? Does the shepherd make the sheep sleep outside the fold? No! What does the shepherd do? He restores them.

How does the shepherd restore them? Lovingly! They don't come sneaking into the fold with their tails between their legs. They are the center of rejoicing. The shepherd is happy, and the other sheep know the shepherd would do the same for them, so they are happy too.

Lord, thank You for forgiving me when I stray.

After the Shepherd finds you, you can joyfully testify, "He restores my soul." You are returned to the fold with the other sheep. You are given green pastures from which to eat and still waters that furnish cool drink. You can lie down happy right next to the Shepherd, because He restores your soul.

Your Turn to Pray

Lord, several times in my life I've wandered from You, and I didn't even know what I was doing. Thank You for coming after me to restore my soul.

Lord, I never intended to stray from You, but I did. Thank You for bringing me back to the fold.

Lord, I'm sorry for my wandering feet. Forgive my sin and keep me close to You.

Are you running on empty? Is there still a sense of purpose to your life? Do you have a compelling reason to get out of bed each morning? Some people just travel from home to work and back again. They occasionally go to the movies. They take a vacation once a year. They sometimes visit relatives. But they have no purpose in life!

Like the Miss America candidate who, when asked about her purpose in life, answered, "Just to have fun," some people think the purpose of life is to entertain themselves. Beyond having fun, they enjoy little in the way of deep satisfaction, and they can point to few accomplishments. They're not serving God. They're not trying to make the world a better place. They're not trying to improve themselves. They just live from event to event.

Have you ever needed restoration in your physical body? Remember the last time you were sick—a hacking cough, fever or even diarrhea? You felt terrible. You didn't want to go to work, eat or play golf. You felt so bad, you couldn't sleep. But eventually you *did* sleep; and when you woke up, you felt better. The fever had broken, and your body was restored. In the same way, the Shepherd can restore a wandering soul. He can give you spiritual health.

Lord, I want to be strong.

Has your commitment to God slipped? Maybe there's a site on the Internet that you visit, though you know you shouldn't. When you type in the web address, you can smell the aroma of rotting flesh—yours. Then you hit the "enter" key and open the forbidden door.

Sometimes you slip away from God and you need to be restored. What can you do? There is a biblical way to restoration when you slip.

First, acknowledge to yourself and God that you visited the wrong website (or did something else you knew was wrong). Take responsibility for wandering. Second, ask the Shepherd to forgive you.

If we confess our sins, He is faithful and just to forgive us our sins and to cleanse us from all unrighteousness (1 John 1:9).

Next, you must repent of your rebellion and commit yourself never to go there again. Finally, to walk in victory you must continuously surrender the problem to God, and you need to find at least one other person who will hold you accountable.

The Shepherd picks up your spirit and makes you look forward to a new day.

Maybe you haven't slipped outwardly. Maybe you're just spiritually tired. Remember the time you ached because you worked too long in the yard? You could barely get out of bed the next morning. You went to work tired, and you didn't want to face the day's activities. What you needed then was physical restoration.

Sometimes you're so worn out that you just don't want to pray, read the Bible or go to church. You don't have any ambition to do anything for God. The problem is probably not sin; it's just that you are physically exhausted.

Lord, give me physical rest for spiritual restoration.

When you're physically down, what gets you up? For some, it's coffee. For others, it's a long nap. For others still, it's exercise or a protein shake. Some of us bounce back when we hear good news. And still others are restored by a telephone call from a sweetheart or an e-mail bringing good news.

Sometimes when you're spiritually down, look in the Word of God for good news. When the Bible says, "He restores my soul," it means that the Shepherd picks up your spirit and makes you look forward to a new day.

Lord, I expect this day will be better than the last.

Sometimes when sheep wander from their shepherd, they come to a place where the grass is dry, dead or nonexistent. Without food, they grow weak. Sometimes a hot wind saps their strength; other times the blistering sun steals their stamina. So what does the shepherd do? He leads his sheep under the shade of the palm trees near cool water. The shepherd makes them lie down in green pastures to restore the soul of his sheep.

How does the Shepherd restore your soul? Does the Shepherd use good news, a hot meal, coffee or an unexpected phone call? Mostly the Shepherd uses spiritual resources such as the Word of God, prayer, Christian fellowship and worship. As you rest in the Lord, the Shepherd will restore your soul.

Do you remember when you loved the Lord so much that you did not consider it a sacrifice to get up early to pray or go to church? You just *had* to be there. Remember when you used to memorize verses, share the gospel with lost people and sing hymns and worship songs with intense passion?

But then something happened. Perhaps you didn't sin outright or run after the things of this world. Your spiritual temperature may have cooled when your job needed more attention, the kids needed more time or you gave more attention to your hobby than to serving the Lord. Maybe when you came back from vacation you didn't get as involved in church, and you decided not to teach Sunday School that year. Now that your faith is famished, what you need is for the Shepherd to restore your soul.

Lord, bring me back.

What does the word "restore" mean? *To make new.* One of the recent Bible translations reads, "He renews my strength" (Psalm 23:3, *NLT*). When you restore the paint on your car, it looks like new; and when you run your hand over the surface, it feels as good as new. When the Lord restores your soul, you're like new—you have a new start or a new beginning.

When the Lord restores your soul, He renews your strength and makes you feel like you did when you were first saved. Remember that feeling? You laughed . . . you cried . . . you rejoiced. And with new spiritual energy you genuinely believed, "I can do all things through Christ who strengthens me" (Philippians 4:13). Life was sweet when you were first saved, when heaven was real to you. That's the way you'll feel when the Lord restores your soul.

What do you do when you are physically tired? You look forward to the weekend when you can recharge your "battery." You need physical and emotional strength to return to the daily grind. You need the weekend to revive your frayed emotions. With other people, it's their spirit: They don't like their work, and they just don't want to go back.

But the problem may run even deeper than that: You *hate* to go to work. You drag yourself out of bed, you take every sick day possible, and even on the job you give it your second best. You know you could do better, but you just don't. You need renewal.

Savvy managers understand that people need incentives to stay sharp at work: a raise, a promotion, a transfer, stock options or a new challenge. Just as a wise boss knows how to restore the soul of her workers, so the wise Shepherd knows how to restore the soul of His sheep.

Lord, restore me even when I don't seek it.

When the Shepherd says He restores your soul, what does the word "soul" mean to you? It's more than restoring your mind, for your soul is more than your thought patterns. Your soul includes the mind but is much deeper. Your mind expresses itself through thoughts, and your mind communicates with others through words. But your soul is the part of you that creates words, thoughts and ideas.

Your soul is also more than just your emotions. When you say, "I love you with all my heart," you are expressing the warm feelings of your soul. Your deep love commitments come from your emotions, but your soul is more than those fiery emotions of love and jealousy and those black feelings of hate. Your emotions serve to ventilate your soul, but your soul is more than your emotions.

Going deep within, you will find that your will, the power to make decisions, is also an instrument of your soul. Your dreams, your values, the attitudes that influence your everyday life—these are all expressions of the soul. The soul is who you are when no one else is around. When you really get dissatisfied with yourself, remember, "He restores my soul."

I have strayed like a lost sheep. Seek your servant, for I have not forgotten your commands (Psalm 119:176, *NIV*).

My soul is the power within me that relates to God. It is the window through which I see God and allow Him to see me.

My soul is the monitor that tells me whether I am spiritually hot or cold. It is the thermostat that cools my anger or heats up my love.

My soul is the song of my heart and the fragrance of my attitude. It reflects the shadows of my character.

My soul is me, and God can restore me.

Lord, restore my soul.

Your Turn to Pray

Lord, I'm not sure what is in my soul.
I want to love You more but I don't. I want to serve You more,
but I hold back. Forgive me and turn me to You.
Lord, look into my soul and show me what You see. I feel out
of touch with You and need You to restore my soul.
Lord, my soul is empty. I don't love You as much as I once did,
nor do I serve You as I once did. Restore my soul
to love and service.

CHAPTER SIX

HE LEADS ME IN THE PATHS OF RIGHTEOUSNESS

Why does the Lord lead you to green pastures and still waters? Because He loves you and cares that your needs are satisfied.

Lord, thank You for loving me and caring for me.

Why does the Lord protect you from the dangers of temptation and evil? Because He is a holy God who will punish sin.

Lord, thank You for forgiving me and keeping me from judgment.

Why does the Lord lead you in paths of righteousness? Because He is righteous and wants you to be like Him. He wants you to think right, live right and decide right. The Lord wants you to walk rightly in the right paths.

What the Shepherd wants for you, He wants for all His sheep.

> The LORD is my Shepherd;
>   I shall not want.
> He makes me lie down in green pastures
>   For rest and restoration.
> He leads me in right paths
>   (Psalm 23:1-3, author's paraphrase).

We often wander through life wondering, *Where am I to go? How do I get there? What do I do when I arrive? Why am I even going?* All these questions are answered by the Shepherd. He knows what is best for you.

But like many sheep, you sometimes think you have a better idea how to run your life, so you don't always follow the

Shepherd's leading. But before you take your eyes off the Shepherd and begin walking away from His right paths, consider this: You don't know what will happen tomorrow . . . or next week . . . or next year. You can't predict the future. But the Shepherd can.

He said, "I am the Alpha and the Omega, the Beginning and the End" (Revelation 1:8). He knows exactly what will happen tomorrow, so He is qualified to be the perfect guide for your life. Let Him lead you. When you can't trust the Lord with your future, it's called *unbelief.* Do you have a doubting heart?

Some don't trust Him with their future because they know they can't play around with sin if He is in control. If you won't trust Him, it's called *rebellion.* Do you have a sinful heart?

It's unbelief when you *can't* trust the Lord.

It's rebellion when you *won't* trust the Lord.

The Shepherd leads us to right paths because we don't know where we are going. Think for a moment about all the things you must do today. You have errands to run, family responsibilities and obligations at work. After that, you may have things to do for the church, your kids' sports teams or your friends. Then there are the things you do for yourself—education, entertainment, hobbies or self-improvement. You will do what you have to do, but are you doing what you should do for God? Will you trust the Shepherd and follow Him along the right paths?

Lord, be my Shepherd and lead me to do the right things.

You are doing a lot of things, but are you doing them "rightly"? In this busy life, we have so much to do that we give a lot of things a lick and a promise. Are you halfheartedly giving halftime to your projects? When it comes to the church, do you give much effort? Oftentimes in our busyness we don't pray effectively, we don't study the Bible deeply, and we don't serve with excellence. We need the Shepherd to guide us in order to walk rightly on the right paths.

Lord, I need to do things better.

Like sheep, we go through life looking for something to eat. If we don't lift our heads to look around, we will end up eating sour food or poison grass. Lift your head, spot the Shepherd and let Him lead you on right paths to better food and pure water. He knows what's best for you.

Lord, I didn't realize I was lost until I found myself in trouble. Lead me back to the right paths.

Just because you let the Shepherd lead you years ago doesn't mean you can find your way today. Sheep are constantly drawn toward dangerous cliffs and treacherous paths. Are you just like them, going through life playing too close to the edge? Do you get hurt because you don't let the Shepherd lead you?

Lord, I've been hurt. Don't let it happen again.

The shepherd is like a guide, taking the sheep where they ought to go. And what are the qualifications for a guide? He's been there before and knows how to get his sheep to green pastures. He knows the safest paths. Best of all, he knows what is waiting for the sheep when they get to their destination. So the shepherd gathers his sheep together to lead them, guide them and go before them to greener pastures.

Lord, I want to follow You because I want something better in my life.

Where does the Shepherd lead you? He leads you in paths of righteousness. While the word "righteousness" scares many, it simply means that He leads you in the right paths. Technically, these paths conform to the right things God wants done. And if they are done right for God, then they will be right for you.

Notice the Shepherd doesn't necessarily lead us in easy paths, beautiful paths or even prosperous paths. While right paths may be desirable at times, and often there are observation points from which to see the beautiful sights in this world, sometimes right paths are hard to walk. Sometimes we must walk through difficulties and tragedies. Sometimes the Shepherd has to lead you up steep slopes through rocks. The right path can be a difficult path.

Doing the right thing has to do with character. But how do we define character? (So few people today have it.) Character is habitually doing the right thing in the right way. The Shepherd will always lead you to do the right thing in the right way. He will never lead you to the wrong destination, nor will He teach you to do things the wrong way. He will lead you rightly so you will develop the habit of doing things His way.

Remember, the Shepherd doesn't lead you in right paths just to please Himself, although the Shepherd does do it for His name's sake. He has you on the right path for *your* good. The Shepherd has a plan to work all things together for good. The paths He chooses for you are for your good as well as for His good purpose.

Your Turn to Pray
Lord, I see You up ahead, I know where You are going.
But sometimes I fall behind, and it's difficult to follow.
Help me obey.
Lord, I get mixed up at times. I think I'm doing the
right things, but I get lost on the wrong paths. Help me see
You clearly and follow You closely.
Lord, I know it's good for me to follow You, but help me
obey for more than selfish reasons. Help me to please
You by walking in right paths.

Psalm 23 describes the Shepherd *leading* His sheep, not *driving* them. Why? When a shepherd uses his staff to drive his sheep toward a certain destination, they scatter in all directions.

We all, like sheep, have gone astray, each of us has turned to his own way (Isaiah 53:6, *NIV*).

Sheep are not smart enough to understand that the shepherd is herding them to good pastures or cool water. Sheep have minds of their own.

Lord, I'm stubborn and rebellious. Forgive me when I refuse to follow right paths.

Shepherds in David's day didn't round up sheep the way a cowboy rounds up cattle into a corral or pen. Sheep weren't fenced in for feeding and watering. The shepherd led his sheep from one pasture to another so they could feed themselves.

Look again at the text: The shepherd doesn't transport his sheep from one place to another in a wagon or truck. No! The sheep walk from one place to another. The shepherd walks before them, leading them to the next place of food, knowing the only way to get the sheep to a green pasture is to lead them there. Remember, the key to your spiritual life is a correct relationship with the Shepherd. You must follow where He leads. When you are in right relationship to the Lord, He will lead you to the place of food and rest.

Psalm 23 doesn't show us the shepherd telling his sheep where to go. No, that would also be useless. The shepherd can point with his staff, but the sheep won't understand his motions. The shepherd can speak, yell or even gesture, but sheep don't understand gestures. Sheep understand one thing: example. They follow where the shepherd goes. Where is your Shepherd leading you today?

Maybe you don't know where He's going, but are you willing to follow Him anywhere? Your Shepherd may be leading you toward a dark valley filled with frightening death shadows. If He is leading you toward a storm, it's for a purpose. Green pastures lie just on the other side of the threatening valley. Are you willing to follow?

Today the Shepherd may be leading you in easy paths with bright sunny days. But out in the future there is a black valley for you. Just remember: On the other side, your Shepherd is preparing a table spread with food. Are you willing to follow Him?

Your Turn to Pray

*Lord, I know You are up front leading me, but I am hardhead-
ed and selfish. Make me follow You even when I don't want to.
Lord, You're leading me through some dark valleys and I'm
afraid. Remind me of the destination and keep me close to You.
Lord, I have a hard time accepting the sickness and death
of those I love; it hurts to lose them. Help me see the right paths
You've chosen for them and for me.*

Have you realized that your Shepherd won't always tell you how
to walk and when to follow Him? That's something you already
know. He just expects you to do it. Many times your Shepherd
won't tell you where He is going; He just expects you to follow
Him. Are you willing to obey your Shepherd even when you
don't know where He's going?

Lead on, Lord. I will follow.

Your Shepherd will not sneak off in the night, leaving you
alone. Your Shepherd will not play hide-and-seek with you. The
Lord is your Shepherd, and He is ever present to lead you in
paths of righteousness. If your shepherd gets lost from time to
time, then your shepherd is not the Lord. And if your shepherd
does not lead you in paths of righteousness, again, your shep-
herd is not the Lord.

When you think about paths of righteousness, where do you
think they lead? Some people think the Lord will only lead us to
Sunday School or to worship services. Others think the Lord
also leads us to revival meetings or a Christian camp. Usually
people associate some form of religious service with paths of
righteousness. But that's not it.

The paths of righteousness are everyday trails. Some lead to
the grocery store. Some lead down to the expressway to work.
Other right paths are taken by planes and trains.

It's not only *where* the Shepherd leads you, it's *how* He leads
you and *when*. If the Lord is your Shepherd, he wants to lead you

all the time, to every location, by many different means of transportation. It means the Shepherd wants to lead your outward obedience and your inward attitude. When you are following the right paths, you have the right responses of mind, will and emotions.

Learn to go where the
Shepherd leads.

Some translate "paths of righteousness" to mean a good path or the easiest path or the desirable path. The purpose of life is not to go where you want to go; you must learn to go where the Shepherd leads.

There may be more than one trail going up the side of the mountain, with some sheep on the upper trail and some sheep on a lower trail. Which one is right for you? When you follow the Shepherd, He leads you in right paths. This means some paths are right for you, right for this time or right for this place. Don't get envious or jealous of other sheep on other paths. What may be the right path for them could be the wrong path for you.

Lord, help me follow the right path You have chosen for me.

The way God has gifted you determines how your Shepherd will lead you. Your right path may be behind a desk, but another who works well with his hands will be led by the Shepherd to the assembly line or a construction site. The Shepherd has a right path for a good manager that may be different from the one He has chosen for a good teacher.

Lord, what's my gift?

A minister must follow the Shepherd on right paths for the ministry, and a mother must follow right paths for training her children. There are right paths for janitors, farmers and engineers. What is the best path for you? Only one person knows what is best for you: your Shepherd. And to find the right path for you, you must get close to your Shepherd and let Him lead you constantly.

Lord, I realize You have a right path for me. Help me find it and follow it.

If there are right paths, then there are also wrong paths. Proverbs 14:12 says, "There is a way that seems right to a man, but its end is the way of death." You may think you are following right paths because of momentary success or excitement, but do you know whether your path leads to life or death? Is there a green pasture in your future? Will you dwell in the house of the Lord forever?

You can't always tell if your path is a right path by looking down at your feet. Your feet may feel like they're on the right path, but feelings are deceptive. You could be going in the wrong direction. Make sure you are on the right path; look at the horizon toward your destination. Where are you heading? Unless the Lord is your Shepherd, you probably don't understand the future, nor will you reach the right destination.

Lord, lead my feet to the right destination.

Some Old Testament scholars teach that right paths mean *straight* paths—not straight without a curve, but straight according to God's standard. In other words, live straight, think straight and act straight. When the Lord is your Shepherd, He will lead you in straight paths. What's the opposite of a straight path? A crooked one! If you are being led down a crooked path, then the Lord is not your Shepherd. Check your footprints. You can tell a lot about your direction by looking back at where you've been walking. Look in the rearview mirror to see if you are walking straight according to the Word of God. The Lord will lead you in straight paths, which means you will habitually do the right thing in the right way.

What kind of paths are you seeking? Exotic paths? Fun paths? Successful paths? Prosperous paths? Power paths? There are all kinds of paths that you can tread upon in this life, and sheep who don't look around can easily get lost. If you are lost and you are not sure where you are going, you need to lift your head. Look first at the Shepherd before you look down at your feet, then look back to check your bearings. And finally, look to the destination; look to the future.

You may think you're on a good path, but you don't know what the Shepherd knows. Unless you follow the Lord as your Shepherd, you will miss the right path for you.

Your Turn to Pray

Lord, I know You lead me to church and to pray. Help me see
the right paths You've chosen for my life outside the church.
Lord, I know there are right paths and wrong paths. Help me
recognize the difference and choose the right one.
Lord, sometimes when I am following the right path, it leads
through a dark, frightening valley. Stay close to me. Lead me to
green pastures and protect me.

CHAPTER SEVEN

FOR HIS NAME'S SAKE

I learned early the importance of a family name. Because our family name was important to my mother, it became important to me. My mother was the tenth child born to Eula and Robert McFaddin of Clarendon County, South Carolina. Originally, the land in the county was given as a grant by the king of England to the McFaddins during colonial times.

When I was a young boy, my mother stood me before a 10-foot-tall granite stone in the McFaddin Cemetery. The stone traced the family lineage all the way back to the original John McFaddin, who first carved a farm out of the wilderness. Mother told me of my ancestors fighting off Indian raids and later fending off the British during the American Revolution. She pointed at the names of my ancestors, carved in granite. She said, "One day your name will be carved in granite stone somewhere. You're a Towns." She transposed my loyalty from her maiden name to her married name. "Make me proud of you."

She constantly reminded me during my childhood that I had her blood flowing through my veins. "You're a Towns. You can do anything you set your mind to do," she would say. Little did I realize at the time that my mother was planting the seeds of dreams in my heart that would grow to influence my adult actions. I tried not to act "ugly" (a southern expression for naughty behavior) because I was a Towns. Because of my mother's expectations, I tried to overcome seemingly insurmountable obstacles when I found myself in difficult circumstances. I wanted to make my parents proud of me.

In the same way, the Lord wants us to meet His expectations and to live for Him for His name's sake.

THE SHEPHERD'S MANY NAMES

The LORD is my shepherd;
(*Jehovah-Roi*, my Protector)

I shall not want.
(*Jehovah-Jireh*, my Provider)

He makes me to lie down in green pastures;
(*Jehovah-Adonai*, my Master)

He leads me beside the still waters.
(*Jehovah-Shalom*, my Peace)

He restores my soul;
(*Jehovah-Rophi*, my Healer)

He leads me in the paths of righteousness for His name's sake.
(*Jehovah-Tsidkenu*, my Righteousness)

Yea, though I walk through the valley of the shadow of death,
(*Jehovah-Shammah*, my divine Presence)

I will fear no evil; for You are with me;
(*Jehovah-Tsebaoth*, my Warrior)

Your rod and Your staff, they comfort me.
(*Jehovah-El Elyon*, my Defender)

You prepare a table before me in the presence of my enemies;
(*Jehovah-Nissi*, my Encourager)

You anoint my head with oil;
(*Jehovah-Mekaddesh*, my Righteousness)

My cup runs over.
(*Jehovah-El Shaddai*, my Nourisher)

Surely goodness and mercy shall follow me all the days of my life;
(*Jehovah-El Elohim*, my Protector)

And I will dwell in the house of the LORD forever.
(*Jehovah-El Olam*, my Eternity)

He leads me in right paths, for the sake of His many names (Psalm 23:3, author's paraphrase).

Shepherds risk their lives to protect their sheep because losing a sheep is like losing a part of themselves. A shepherd loves his sheep, and he will risk everything for them. His love motivates him to learn all about sheep and how to care for them, because it's not just an occupation. Each sheep is a part of his heart. He knows their weaknesses and which ones tend to stray. He knows the strengths of those that remain close to him. He knows what they like to eat and what they shouldn't eat. It's a shepherd's nature to know such things.

Lord, You know me.

The shepherd takes pride in the health and safety of his flock. He knows it's a dereliction of his duty if any sheep are hurt by wolves or if any wander off and are killed. A shepherd knows he must supervise everything his sheep do at every moment of the night and day. If he doesn't do a good job, the shepherd knows he has failed his family or his employer. But most of all, the shepherd has failed himself.

The shepherd takes ownership of his sheep, even if he is tending the flock for his father or master. He loves even the smallest sheep, protecting it as his own life and tenderly nurturing it to full health and strength. The shepherd and sheep are one. He puts his name and reputation on the flock collectively and on each sheep individually.

Lord, thank You for owning me.

Why does the shepherd sacrifice for his sheep, even when it means risking his life? For the sake of his name. Because the shepherd has identified with the sheep, if something happens to them it happens to him. When the shepherd fails, he has lost the respect of others. But most of all, he has lost his self-respect, and in his eyes he is a failure.

I praise You, eternal Shepherd, for never failing.

When the psalmist says the Shepherd does everything for His name's sake, it means the Shepherd cares for His sheep because that's who He is and that's what He does. Shepherding is his nature. There's an old saying, "What's in the cup passes through the lips." What's in the Shepherd's heart comes out in His actions. The Shepherd loves His sheep because He is our loving Lord. The Shepherd loves you because of who He is. It's all for the sake of His name.

When you say "The Lord is my Shepherd," you are saying in Hebrew *Jehovah-Roi*. This is one of the names of God. This name suggests that the Lord is powerful to protect His sheep from danger. But the name also means the Lord is tender to care for them and provide for their every need.

Jehovah-Roi, protect me from evil.

Because the Lord has a shepherd's heart, He wants you to have the best to eat and drink. Have you been hungry lately? Perhaps you've strayed from the Shepherd's fold and you are eating old, dead, dried-up grass. That's not what the Shepherd has for you. Remember, Psalm 23 is about *relationship*, and if you remain in the fold—and if you stay near the Shepherd—you will have good food.

> Oh, taste and see that the LORD is good; blessed is the
> man who trusts in Him! (Psalm 34:8).

The Shepherd will provide you with good food for the sake of His name.

Lord, let me eat near You.

Because the Lord is your Shepherd, you can now say, "I shall not want." When you think of God's provision, think of His name *Jehovah-Jireh*, which means, "The Lord Is My Provider" (see Genesis 22:14). Jehovah-Jireh provided Israel with food for 40 years as they wandered in the desert wilderness. Jehovah-Jireh also provided Israel with water from a rock when there was no water in the desert (see Numbers 20:7-11). The very nature of a shepherd is Jehovah-Jireh, to be a provider. If Jehovah-Jireh can do that for so many people (more than one million) for so long, what can He do for you? Jehovah-Jireh will provide for you. Why? For His name's sake.

Thank You, Jehovah-Jireh, for everything.

Because the Lord is your Shepherd, He makes you lie down in green grass. He is *Jehovah-Adonai,* your Master, which means He knows what is best for you. Even more, the Master wants obedience and knows if you are lying in green grass and if you are close to His feet. Why does He make you lie down? The Shepherd wants you to have rest and peace.

You will finally have peace ❧ when you intimately know the Shepherd. ❧

That's why He has another name, *Jehovah-Shalom,* meaning "The Lord Is Peace" (see Judges 6:24). When you lie serenely beside still waters, thank God for providing you with peace in a world where there is so little peace. The Shepherd's name is "The Prince of Peace" (Isaiah 9:6, *KJV*). You will finally have peace when you intimately know the Shepherd.

Jehovah-Shalom, thank You for rest of heart that You give me because of Your name's sake.

Maybe you are one of the sheep that likes to see what enticements lie in other pastures. Have you been running ahead of the Shepherd? Maybe you are the sheep that likes thrills and excitement. You are a "party sheep," and you've been straying into dangerous mountain trails. You've even gone some places where there are no paths, and you've fallen a few times. Now you are bruised and battered.

You need to know the Shepherd's name, *Jehovah-Rophi*. That means "The Lord Is My Healer" (see Exodus 15:26). When the Shepherd finds you, does He punish you for going to the wrong places? No! The Shepherd restores you to the flock; you are brought back with the other sheep. Why does He forgive you and restore you? Because His name is Jehovah-Rophi; He is a healer and restorer.

Jehovah-Rophi, keep me from disease and heal me in sickness.

Now it is the season when the Shepherd must move the sheep from one pasture to another. There are many paths and you could get lost if you don't stay close to the Shepherd. Some would like to stay in the old pastures, but there is no food in old pastures; sheep will eat grass right down to the roots. After a period of time you must be moved to a new pasture of fresh green grass, and you can't find the way by yourself.

The Shepherd will lead you in paths of righteousness. Why? Because He is *Jehovah-Tsidkenu*, which means "The Lord, Our Righteousness." When you broke His laws, the Lord substituted Himself on the cross at Calvary for your punishment because He is righteous. Then the Lord gave you His righteousness so you would be perfect (see Matthew 5:48; Hebrews 10:14). Now you can walk in the paths of righteousness because of the sake of His name.

Jehovah-Tsidkenu, thank You for making me righteous.

Some refuse to walk in right paths but instead choose to walk through the valley of the shadow of death. Are you in a black valley? You've created this mess by yourself, but don't fear. Even in the valley, the Bible promises, "You are with me" (Psalm 23:4). Why would the Shepherd go after you when you're in trouble? Because that's His nature. He's *Jehovah-Shammah*, which means "The Lord Is There," or "The Lord Is with Me." The Lord is with you in the dark valley because of the sake of His name.

Jehovah-Shammah, be with me even to the ends of the earth.

What's chasing you in the valley? Is there a death shadow pursuing you like a lioness running down an antelope? Do you feel a demon from hell nipping at your heels? You are running as fast as you can, but the death shadow is gaining ground. When you feel like you are almost being eaten alive, remember His name *Jehovah-Tsebaoth,* "The Lord, My Warrior." The Lord will fight for you in the black valley, because that's His name.

Lord, come quickly. I'm losing; please fight for me.

If you've lost a battle, lift up your head to see the Shepherd running to your rescue. He has a rod and staff to protect you. Why does He carry you? Because His name is *Jehovah-El Elyon,* which means "The Lord God Most High," or "The Lord God, My Defender" (see Genesis 14:22). He protects you because His name says He will.

Jehovah-El Elyon, I am confident in Your care.

When you come out of death's dark valley, what's waiting for you? Not punishment—just the opposite. The Shepherd has a table loaded with good food waiting for you—cheese, meats, ripe fruit and delectable desserts. The Shepherd will feed you in the presence of your enemies (see Psalm 23:5) to demonstrate that He can both provide for you and protect you.

So eat all you want. Why? Because His name is *Jehovah-Nissi,* which means "The Lord, My Banner" (see Exodus 17:15), or "The Lord Who Rallies Us to Himself." After a battle the troops rally around their standard, or banner. But as Christians we don't rally around a flag fluttering in the breeze; we get close to the Shepherd, where our hope is restored after the battle. We want Him to know we are grateful. He lets us get close because of His name.

Jehovah-Nissi, it's been tough. Can I get closer?

When you are wounded in the battle, He anoints your head with oil (see Psalm 23:5). The Shepherd douses you with cleansing oil to remove impurities from your wounds, and He anoints you with healing oil to make you healthy again. Why does the Shepherd do this? Because His name is also *Jehovah-Mekaddesh*, which means "The Lord Who Sanctifies" or "The Lord Who Makes You Righteous." It's His nature.

Jehovah-Mekaddesh, I am honored to be Your sheep.

Look down the table. The Shepherd is filling your cup—not someone else's cup—to the brim. Notice that your cup is not partially filled. The Lord is pouring so much into your chalice that it is beginning to overflow. Wow! Now you realize the Shepherd loves you and treats you special. Why is He doing this for you? Because that's the way He does things. His name is *Jehovah-El Shaddai*, which means "The Lord, My Nourisher" (see Genesis 17:1,2). The Lord loves to give thirsty people something to drink. He is the almighty One who supplies all your needs.

Jehovah El-Shaddai, fill my cup.

As the Shepherd leads you from one pasture to another, you don't have to worry about death shadows tracking you down. When you follow the Shepherd's leadership, His "goodness and mercy" will follow you (Psalm 23:6). Why? Because He is *Jehovah-El Elohim*, which means "The Lord God Is Strong to Protect" (Joshua 22:22). The Shepherd looks after His sheep because His reputation is at stake. He will protect you for His name's sake.

Jehovah-El Elohim, I rest in Your protection.

The shepherd would prefer to live in a house, away from the rain and wind and protected from the snow. He wants an abode where no snakes or scorpions can slip under his tent or crawl under his blanket. So here's good news: The Shepherd is going home and taking His sheep with Him! The sheep are going to live in a house, but not just any house. They will live in God's house! And the greatest thing about God's house is that He lives there.

Why does the Shepherd take His sheep to His eternal home? Because His name is *Jehovah-El Olam*, which means "The Lord God of Eternity" (see Psalm 48:14). Some scholars translate this

"The Lord God of His Secrets." The Hebrew word *olam* can be translated either "eternity" or "secret," which might suggest that the Lord God has many secret things to share with you when you get to His house. Why would He do that? Because the Shepherd's name is Jehovah-El Olam. He will take you to live with Him forever—because of His name's sake.

Your Turn to Pray

*Lord, I didn't know You had so many names. Help me know
You better through all Your names.
I thank You for everything Your names mean to me.
Lord, Your many names tell me about the different things You
do for me. Help me understand every way You help me.
Keep helping me; there's a lot more I need.
Lord, I worship You for Your power and greatness.
I marvel at Your care and concern for me. I accept Your
forgiveness and restoration.*

PART 2

WHAT HIS SHEEP RECEIVE

The relationship between the sheep and the Shepherd is two-way. In the first half of the psalm, we see all the great things our Lord does for us, without us having to do anything.

The second half of Psalm 23 is the "I" section. Because the Shepherd has done everything for me, I am now responsible to follow Him closely so He can provide for me and protect me. What does this mean for me, His sheep?

I will fear no evil.

I will have Him with me always.

I will be comforted by His rod and staff.

I will eat from a prepared table.

I will have my head anointed with oil.

I will have goodness and mercy follow me.

I will dwell in the house of the Lord forever.

CHAPTER EIGHT

YEA, THOUGH I WALK THROUGH THE VALLEY OF THE SHADOW OF DEATH

Shadows scared me nearly to death when I was a youngster. Because we lived next to a cemetery, I believed that the threat of spirits from dead bodies was ever present. But it was the threat of live burglars that frightened me most.

The moon shining through our pear tree caused strange shadows to dance on the cheap paper shade that covered my bedroom window. I was certain the shadows were those of a robber trying to break into my room. The wind outside made the "burglar shadows" jump, and the limbs scratching on the screen frightened me even more. My mouth would turn to cotton, so I couldn't yell for mother, and I was too scared to move. I would sweat, vowing not to move, so the burglar would think I was asleep.

The next morning—an eternity later!—I would wake up and everything would be all right.

Yea, though I walk through the valley of the shadow of death, I will fear no evil; for You are with me (Psalm 23:4).

Even when walking through a dark, dangerous valley, I will not be scared of death shadows, because You are with me (Psalm 23:4, author's paraphrase).

Up until now the Shepherd has been leading you. He always leads His sheep to a grassy pasture and a pool of still water. So how did you end up in a dark valley full of shadows and death? The Lord didn't lead you there. You *chose* the path of darkness . . . the path of shadows . . . the path of death. Notice that the psalm declares, "Yea, though I walk through the valley." There's no Shepherd out in front. You chose the valley because you strayed from the Shepherd.

> Into the ever-increasing darkness descents
>   Is not a place the Shepherd sends.
> Into the deepening dark night of the soul,
>   Until the Shepherd brings us back to the fold.

What is scary about valleys are the high mountains on either side of the path. You can get lost among high mountains because the alpine passes are always turning to the right or left. Sometimes they seem to turn completely around! Then you've lost your sense of direction for sure.

Lord, give me direction in the mazelike valleys of life.

Sometimes you are following a valley through high, foreboding mountains—then you come to a dead end. You are stranded in a box canyon with no way out. Have you ever been frustrated because a mountain blocked your path? Here's what you do when blocked by a mountain. First, remember that the Lord is in the mountain-moving business. If you have faith the size of a small seed, you can say to your mountain barrier, "Get out of the way!" and it will be removed (see Matthew 17:20).

You don't need to be hemmed in by mountains. Remove them by faith. But sometimes you don't have much faith, much less enough faith to move mountains. So what can you do?

Try the second option. When you come to the end of your path in a box canyon, turn around. The path that led you into the valley can lead you out. When you turn around to go in the opposite direction, that's called repentance. The path that you followed away from the Shepherd also leads you back to Him. It runs both ways.

Lord, help me stay on the path. I'm coming back home!

Then there are wrong paths in the valley. Because the mountains are high all around you, it's easy to follow the wrong path in the valley. And what happens when you do? You end up at the wrong destination. When you thought getting drunk was cool because all your friends were doing it, you never thought you

ℰ Remember, the Lord is in the mountain-moving business. ℰ

would end up hooked. Now you're addicted. Maybe not to alcohol, but to sex, drugs, food, sports or TV. There are a lot of good things that will hook you if you're not close to the Shepherd. If you've taken the wrong path down the wrong valley, do what a lost lamb does: It cries. Cry out to the Shepherd who can free you and bring you back to green pastures and pools of still water!

Lord, "unhook" me from addictive things.

You can be blinded by the dazzling sunlight
Or by the foreboding dark night.

Are you walking in a shadow today? How dark are your shadows? Remember, the Shepherd is Jesus. He is the light of the world. His light will dissipate any shadow! Whether your shadows are black or just gray, the Shepherd can illuminate your path.

Lord, shine some light over here.

A shadow isn't real; it's only an illusion. When something blocks the light, it makes a shadow. Or worse, when something distorts the light, what happens? Distorted shadows. If a shadow looks like a friendly hand, you reach out to shake it; but your hand is empty. And if the hand looks threatening, as if it is going to choke you, you perspire, your heart beats faster, you might even yell out in fear. The shadow is not real, but the fear it inspires is very real.

Why do shadows scare us? Remember when you walked home from school on a late winter afternoon? The night came early, and the bitter wind cut through your jacket. The streetlight through the bushes created scary goblins in the shadows. Your pulse beat faster, your mouth went dry, and you wanted to run. You thought if you ran quickly past the shadows the boogeyman wouldn't get you.

Why Shadows Scare You:
You're afraid of the unknown.
You feel defenseless.
Your active imagination thinks you'll die there.
You know evil hides in darkness.

A man walked up the gallows to be hung. The noose was tightened around his neck and the executioner said, "I'll give you two choices. You can be hanged right now, or you can go through that door over there." The plain wooden door looked innocent enough, but the prisoner knew they tortured prisoners in the belly of the prison. He was afraid some type of torture was behind the door, so he chose hanging. What he didn't know was that the door led to freedom. Fear of the unknown makes us hurt ourselves.

Walking home through the dark shadows, you may think a mugger is hiding in the darkness. You begin running madly to get away, but you fall. You scratch up a knee and ruin a good pair of pants. It's often been said, "What you don't know can't hurt you," but that's only half right. What you don't know may not hurt you, but it can make you hurt yourself.

Your Turn to Pray

Lord, I am ignorant of all the dangers I face.
Protect me from unseen threats.
Lord, I don't understand all the implications of the trouble
I'm in. Guard me from going deeper into trouble.
Lord, it's dark and I can't see what's ahead.
Guide me through this valley.
Lord, I don't know if tomorrow will be worse or better.
Prepare me to face whatever comes.
Lord, I'm lonely, scared and don't know what to do.
I know You are with me. Help me to see You and
follow You out of this dark valley.

But even though there is probably nothing in the dark shadows, don't play in the darkness. Why? Because men love darkness more than light, as their deeds are evil (see John 3:19). Have you ever thought about how thieves sneak in under the cover of darkness? How houses of ill repute are dimly lit? How more crimes are committed at night than under the glaring sun? We innately know there's a dark side and a light side to our personalities. We are like Jekyll and Hyde or Beauty and the Beast. The Bible calls this condition the "old man" and the "new man" (Colossians 3:9,10). Our evil deeds come from our evil nature, and we don't want anyone to know about the dark side of our personality.

Are you scared of shadows? How about the shadow of death? When you are close to someone dying, his or her shadow falls over you.

For the last five days of my mother's life, I stayed with her, sleeping in the hospital room. I knew she would die soon. Her kidneys, liver and other internal organs were shutting down. Her feet and legs had swelled to twice their normal size. When her hands and wrists became so swollen that the nurse couldn't get the IV into a vein, I knew it was only a matter of time. The swelling made it impossible for the intravenous needle to feed life-sustaining nourishment and medicine into her body.

For five nights I slept beside her bed. It's an excruciating experience to watch your mother die and not be able to do anything about it. I couldn't even muster up the faith to pray for a miracle. The poison was shutting down her organs one at a time. At 5:17 A.M. on May 3, 1999, she sighed deeply and was gone. But I didn't realize she was dead because her eyes were still open.

At 6:00 A.M. I said, "I'm going down to the hospital cafeteria to get a cup of coffee. We'll pray when I get back." But God stopped me in my tracks. I knew I shouldn't go. So I said, "No, let's pray first."

After getting my Bible, I reached out to touch her hand. When I touched her, I knew she was dead. And then I tried but couldn't close her eyes.

For the next 30 minutes I was incoherent. I couldn't speak. I had been brave in the shadow of death for five days. Death hadn't scared me, but now I was no longer standing in death's shadow, because the shadow was gone. The blackness of death visited the room, and her body was getting colder by the minute. Death's shadow became a reality. All I could do was sit there, immobilized in the presence of a dead body.

Thirty minutes later her pastor walked in the room, laid his hand on the bed next to the dead body and announced, "You know she's not here. Your mother is with the Lord."

Instantly, the burden of death lifted. I knew the pastor was right. It's what I had taught all my life: To be absent from the body is to be present with the Lord (see 2 Corinthians 5:8). When the pastor said that, I stepped out of the shadows and into the light.

Remember, the Lord is our light and life. Why should we fear?

Why Does Death Scare Us?
Our physical eyes can't see the other side.
We do not want physical pain.
We do not want to give up anything.
We have not finished all we have set out to do on Earth.
Because of sin, we have doubts.

Psalm 23 doesn't talk about walking through a valley of death; it says you will walk through a valley of *shadows* that are about death. To the unsaved, death is real. But if you walk with the Shepherd, death is only a shadow. Since shadows are created when something obscures the light, your death will obscure the light only for a moment. You will walk into that dark shadow, momentarily losing perspective of what you see in this life. But the instant you lose sight of earthly things, the shadow of death melts in the light of the other side. You walk through a doorway with the Shepherd into the other side.

Are you afraid of dying? Death seems inevitable to us who are alive because everyone we've ever known dies. Besides being real, death is frightening. Even for Christians, death is a fearful thing. We know some who have descended into a valley of pain, and none of us are very good with pain. Others have gone through a long, debilitating illness as their physical body wasted away. They were weak and ugly, and they lost the power of memory. The valley of death scares us all.

Lord, remind me that death is only a shadow.

Death is very real as it chokes the last breath from our bodies. And then we feel the hand of Jesus. He guides us through death to the other side. Jesus said, "I have the keys of Hades and of Death" (Revelation 1:18), so why should we worry? When you are afraid of walking through death's valley, listen for the jingle of the keys. It's Jesus. He's coming to unlock the door to let you into His Father's house.

Lord, thank You that I am not a latchkey child. The light is on at my eternal home, and You will be there to let me in.

Your Turn to Pray
Lord, I know I'll have to die one day (unless You return first),
so prepare me for that experience.
Lord, I'm afraid to die. I don't like physical pain.
Teach me what I need to know about death.
Lord, I don't want want to lose control of my mind and body
due to lingering illness. Nor do I desire an instant death
by accident. I just don't want to die. Help me accept
death's inevitability.
Lord, give me courage to accept pain and faith to see
Your plan. And take me to live with You when I die.
Lord, give me faith to meet You at death's door.
Be with me as I die.
Lord, I trust You for everything, but it's hard to trust
You about life's final experience because I've never been
there before. Renew my hope.
Lord, give me love for family and friends to the end
and faith to live through anything that comes.

Even when you walk in daylight, do you feel something following you? Does it feel like a pit bull is chasing you, nipping at your heels? You feel death shadows following, even in the sun where there are no shadows. A death shadow could simply be your memory of what happened in the dark. Maybe it's guilt that dogs you constantly. No matter how fast you run, a death shadow keeps pursuing you, and you're sure it's gaining.

Death shadows don't bite, but they can do something worse. They can make you bite yourself through guilt and regret. First you take one bite, then another, and finally you chew yourself up into small pieces. A death shadow can make a person kill himself (or herself).

But your death shadows won't kill you; they'll only leave you maimed. Suppose a lion pounced on you and ripped off your arm. For the rest of your life you would have to live with only one arm. You would get along somehow, but you would miss the arm. When a death shadow pounces on you, its teeth do not chew off your arm, but you still live with emotional scars. Your arm is there, but it feels like it's gone, so you go through life fearful, intimidated, even cowardly.

Death shadows don't scare the Lord. Why? He faced death shadows His entire life. Being rejected at birth, He was born in a stable. Even then a death shadow of a cross flashed across His future. The Old Testament had already predicted His death: "He was wounded for our transgressions" (Isaiah 53:5). Jesus always knew how He would die.

As a young man, Jesus was introduced to the world with the words "Behold the Lamb of God" (John 1:29). In Jesus' day, this was the sacrificial language of the Jews. The death shadow of the cross reminded Him of the prophecy, "And as a sheep before its shearers is silent, So He opened not His mouth" (Isaiah 53:7).

The death shadow of the crucifixion followed Jesus throughout His life. What does that mean to you? Your Shepherd dealt with a much worse death shadow than you will ever face. Whereas many of your shadows are not real, the reality of the cross crushed the physical life out of His body. But because Jesus knows about death shadows, He understands your fears and will go with you through the dark valley. He will be with you until you come out on the other side.

Your Turn to Pray

*Lord, teach me to trust You when I'm scared, because You
know how to handle my fears. I need Your strength and peace.
Lord, I want to get rid of all shadows over my life. You lived all*

Your life with the shadow of the cross looming over You.
Help me to live as You lived.
Lord, how did You put up with the constant shadow of death
over Your life? I can't go through life with this tension.
Take away my fears and anguish.
Lord, I know You are not scared of death shadows
because You faced them all. I claim Your victory over
death shadows for my victory.

So what can you do when shadows scare you?

Seek the Lord's presence. He brings light in your darkest night. Then claim again the promise that "You are with me" (Psalm 23:4). Remember, there is no darkness in God's presence, nor is there any shadow. Jesus said, "I am the light of the world. He who follows Me shall not walk in darkness, but have the light of life" (John 8:12).

When entering your personal "death valley," pray. If you find yourself in the middle of a dark night, pray. If you want to get out of the valley, pray.

Trust Him to help you find the path out. If the valley has you hemmed in and the mountains are too high to climb, remember that a valley can be a path through the mountains. If you can't see the other side, keep following the valley. Claim the promise, "You are with me." The Shepherd won't let you get lost.

If you are on the wrong path, turn around. There are usually box canyons and false trails in the mountains. Not all openings between the mountains will get you to the other side. The easy path may not be the right valley, because it may end abruptly. What do you do then? Turn around—repent—and retrace your steps back to the Shepherd.

Know that God will never abandon you. Anticipation can help you mentally prepare for your valley of troubles. God promises that you will walk *through* the valley—not just *into* the valley to be left there, but *through* it to green pastures. If you are in the valley of the shadow of death, remember that God will never abandon you in the valley. He will bring you out to the other side. God promises to be with you through your trouble.

You were afraid your death shadow was a posse from hell. You have been *fear conscious* when you should have been *God conscious*. You've been so worried about the death shadow that you missed the *divine shadow*. Because we always see in life what we look for, if you search for death shadows, that's what you will find. If you seek God, you will see Him. Who is with you in the darkness? It's the Shepherd. Reach up, take His hand and let Him guide you through the valley to the other side.

Thank You, Lord, for leading me through the dark night.

CHAPTER NINE
I WILL FEAR NO EVIL

Sheep walk confidently through the threatening shadows of a valley because their shepherd is with them. When darkness obscures the path, the shepherd guides them. When predators lurk in the shadows of nearby caves, he protects them. If they fall into a crevice, he will rescue them. If they grow hungry or thirsty, he knows where to find green pastures and still waters.

Lord, guide me through life's threatening problems.

When we say, "I will fear no evil," it may sound as if we are trusting in our own courage. But only bullies who don't understand the complexities of life would boast, "I am not afraid of anything." Never could a sheep make that boast, because of all the animals, sheep are among the most helpless. They cannot stand courageously against a lion that could rip them apart with a swat of his mighty paw. Nor can sheep walk fearlessly into battle against any other animal. How could they? They have no weapons—no means to defend themselves and nothing with which to attack their predators.

Yet the Bible tells us that we can say with confidence, "I will fear no evil." Does this mean we, as the Lord's sheep, should never get scared? No! Many sheep have quivered in the face of approaching death. There are many things to be fearful of, but you should never fear evil. If you fear the Lord who is your Shepherd, He will take care of evil.

Does this mean that sheep should have courage? Yes! Because you belong to the Shepherd, you can testify, "I will fear no evil." The Shepherd can fight the lion for you.

Lord, teach me to let You fight my battles.

Sheep spend their days nose down in pastures of fresh, green grass, paying no attention to perimeter defense. Almost anything could destroy them. When a sheep hears the roar of a bear or lion from behind nearby rocks, what does it do? The sheep lifts its head from grazing and looks around to see that the shepherd is nearby. When it sees the shepherd, the sheep calmly goes back to grazing, because the shepherd is close by to protect the sheep.

The Bible describes the devil as a roaring, hungry lion that walks about seeking whom it may devour (see 1 Peter 5:8). Have you heard a lion's roar in your soul lately? Did it send a shiver up your spine? Did you look around to make sure the Lord was nearby to protect you?

Lord, come over here near me.

When you hear the lion roar, can you say, "I will fear no evil"? You can if you are in a right relationship with Jesus, the Shepherd. When you are near to the Lord, you are safe. The question is not whether you can protect yourself from the evil one. The question is, do you belong to the Shepherd? If you do, He can fend off all your enemies.

Your Turn to Pray
Lord, it's very hard for me to say, "I will fear no evil,"
because I have many fears. I am not always sure, nor am
I courageous. Give me Your courage and strength.
Lord, I have some doubts—not about You but rather about my
faith and my ability. Strengthen my faith to believe in You,
and strengthen my courage to trust You.
Lord, I've been hurt by disappointments and failures.
Friends have let me down and there are emotional scars.
Give me faith to trust You for protection.

Jesus said to John on the Isle of Patmos, "Do not be afraid; I am the First and the Last. I am He who lives, and was dead, and behold, I am alive forevermore. Amen. And I have the keys of Hades and of Death" (Revelation 1:17,18). What does this say to you? Jesus holds the keys to death. He knows when you are going to die, and *nothing* can destroy you before that time. Trust the Shepherd to protect you until then and to guide you through the experience.

He has promised:

> In My Father's house are many mansions; if it were not so, I would have told you. I go to prepare a place for you. And if I go and prepare a place for you, I will come again, and receive you to Myself; that where I am, there you may be also (John 14:2,3).

When it comes time to die, look around for the One who has the keys in His hand. Listen for His words as He cries out, "Hold on! I am coming. I'll open heaven's door." Because you already know that you'll go to be with the Lord when you die, you should say, "I will fear no evil."

Your Turn to Pray

*Lord, I know I will die, and I'm not looking forward to it.
As a matter of fact I dread death. Give me courage to face it.
Lord, thank You for the promise that You have the keys to
death. I trust You to receive me at death. I really have no
other hope but to trust You for eternal life.
Lord, I want to say, "I will fear no evil" at death, but it's
hard to trust in an unseen heaven. So teach me to trust in
Christ who dwells in my heart.*

Vance Havner, a Baptist preacher from North Carolina, has said,

> [God] was here before there was any fear; He will be here when all fear has passed away. Let us remember that He saw everything before there was anything. If we could stand aside today and see what He sees, how baseless would be our theories, how excuseless our tears.[1]

Since the Shepherd knows everything from the beginning and what will happen in the end, you ought to feel safe trusting Him with all your life.

You cannot see what God sees, but there is one thing you can do that will help you get rid of fears: Look at them through the eyes of Jesus. He knows all about your fears, and He knows they are nothing. When you look at your fears through His eyes, they seem so small. He is omnipresent and can detect whatever is lurking on the perimeter of your life. He has omniscient knowledge about everything that will happen, so He can guide you to safety. He has omnipotent power to accomplish His will in your life. And when life is over, He will make sure you arrive at your destination in heaven with Him.

Lord, because You know everything, I trust You with my future.

The story is told of a powerful orator who addressed a large audience in Philadelphia. He cried out that Jesus said, "I am Alpha, Omega; the Beginning and the End." Then the minister stopped for oratorical effect, and when he did, all 3,000 people sat on the edge of their seats waiting for his next words. Then a poor woman who trusted Jesus for everything cried out from the balcony, "Yes! And He is everything in between, too!"

Your Shepherd was present at the beginning of your life, and He will be present at the end of your life; but the most important thing to know is that He is present at everything in between, too.

Your Turn to Pray

Lord, thank You for Your omniscient knowledge.
You know everything that will happen to me. Help me to
trust the future You plan for me.
Lord, thank You for Your omnipresent understanding of
the future. When I'm afraid of what's coming, teach me
to trust in You. Help me see the future through Your eyes.
Lord, thank You for Your omnipotent power to do

everything You want to do. Help me to trust in Your ability
to work all things together for Your glory.

When David said, "I will fear no evil," notice the things he left out. He could have said, "I will fear no man," "no circumstance," "no sickness," "no problem," or even "I will not fear death." Why did he single out evil? Because evil comes from the one who wants to harm us. The fear of death can be evil in the hands of Satan; but the event of death may be good in God's hands, for death may stop suffering or loneliness. Death may stop a sinner from further sin that would have brought dire consequences to his family.

All of us must die, but none of us has to fear death because Jesus holds the keys to death. When things get scary and you're afraid of dying, hang on until the One with the keys gets there.

Franklin D. Roosevelt once said, "The only thing we have to fear is fear itself." Actually, the only thing we have to fear is God Himself. Jesus told us, "Do not fear those who kill the body but cannot kill the soul. But rather fear Him who is able to destroy both soul and body in hell" (Matthew 10:28). You are afraid of the wrong thing: You are afraid of the devil, but all he can do is kill the body. You should fear God. He can cast you into hell where body and soul are lost.

Lord, I was afraid of You until the blood of Jesus cleansed me of sin.

Every day I pray the Lord's Prayer, carefully praying through each of the seven petitions. But some days I spend most of my time praying the first and last petition. Why these? The first petition is worship to God: "Hallowed be thy name" (Luke 11:2, KJV). This petition means, "Holy be Your name on Earth in my life, as Your name in heaven is revered." So I use the many names of God to worship Him.[2]

The last petition of the Lord's Prayer is about the devil: "Deliver us from the evil one" (Matthew 6:13). Every day I pray for God to deliver me from the evil one. When I do, then I can confidently say with the psalmist, "I will fear no evil."

Why do I not fear the evil one? Because greater is He who is within me than he who is in the world (see 1 John 4:4). Two little boys were fighting, and the bully threatened the smaller boy. But the spunky little guy didn't back down, saying, "My dad can whip your dad!" So I will fear no evil because my Father in heaven can whip the father of lies from hell.

Your Turn to Pray

Lord, I sometimes fear the wrong things: I fear the devil and his
evil but not You. Forgive me of my blindness and doubt.
Lord, I have fears that I can't explain, except to say they are so
threatening at times. Give me peace and joy.
Lord, when I become more concerned with the devil than with
You, forgive me for not trusting You and obeying You.
Lord, teach me to fear You most of all and take away all fear of
the devil. Help me to honestly confess, "I will fear no evil."

Notes

1. Vance Havner, quoted by R. T. Ketchum, *I Shall Not Want* (Chicago: Moody Press, 1953), pp. 72, 73.
2. For more from Elmer Towns on the Lord's Prayer and the names of God, see the author's books *Praying the Lord's Prayer for Spiritual Breakthrough* (Ventura, CA: Regal Books, 1998) and *My Father's Names* (Ventura, CA: Regal Books, 1993).

CHAPTER TEN

FOR YOU ARE WITH ME

What a wonderful promise: "Thou art with me" (Psalm 23:4, *KJV*). But the promise is even greater when you examine the different places where the Lord goes with you. Most people think of God being near only in church or when we pray. And, of course, we expect the Lord to be with us when we go to present the gospel to the lost or when we perform a good deed of mercy. But Psalm 23 tells us that the Lord is with us both in difficult places and in restful pastures.

The Lord is not a fair-weather friend who jumps ship at the first sign of a storm. Can you think of any person the Lord has ever left? Not me! There are plenty of illustrations in the Bible of people leaving God and for many different reasons. The prodigal son left for the pleasures of sin. King Saul left because of his jealousy of David. Judas left for money. Paul wrote, "Demas has forsaken me, having loved this present world" (2 Timothy 4:10). But the shepherd won't forsake his sheep, and the Lord won't leave you.

Lord, thank You for this promise.

Jesus spent a morning preaching to the multitudes, and then He directed His disciples to head to the other side of the Sea of Galilee. He needed rest. But a storm would hit the lake as the disciples crossed to the other side. Jesus must have known about it; He knows all things. Nevertheless, He sent the disciples into a coming storm. The best part of the story is that Jesus went with them into the storm, even though He was asleep (see Luke 8:22-25).

Have you ever noticed how storms bother us more than they bother the Lord? Jesus knew the storm was coming, but was he concerned? No! He went to sleep. Doesn't that say something about the troubles in your life? Your storms bother you a lot more than they trouble the Lord.

Lord, help me see my storms through Your eyes.

Don't blame the Lord for going to sleep. Preaching takes a lot out of a person, and He had preached all morning. Then there was the warm sun, the gentle breeze and the lapping of the waves against the boat. What fatigued person wouldn't go to sleep under those conditions? But the disciples were in trouble, and the Lord was asleep.

What did the disciples do when the waves became rough? They didn't turn to the Lord for help when the storm suddenly broke around them. They leaned against the oars, they hoisted the sails, they bailed water . . . and bailed water . . . and bailed water. They did everything they could to get out of trouble. That is, they did everything but ask the Lord for help. They reacted probably just like you react when you get into trouble. You do everything you can think of to solve your problem. You forget that the Lord is with you in the boat. You forget that the Lord knows about the storm and that He sent you into the storm. But He is with you.

Lord, let me never forget Your presence is with me when trouble comes.

Only when the disciples asked for help did the Lord awaken and calm the sea. Though the disciples were probably irritated when they yelled, "Master, Master, we are perishing!" (Luke 8:24), at least they went to Jesus with their predicament. Did Jesus care that the disciples were irritated? No. Did He care whether they perished? Yes! He cares for His own.

Lord, thank You for caring for me.

As you walk through the valley of death shadows, has something frightened you? Just as Jesus cared that His disciples were scared in the storm, so He cares about the things that frighten you. After all, you belong to Him. That's one of the reasons Jesus walks with you in the valley—to keep you from being frightened by death shadows.

Your Turn to Pray

Lord, I know there will be storms in the future and I really
don't want to go through them. Let me feel Your

presence in the darkest night.
Lord, when I lose my direction in the darkest storm,
come show Yourself to me. Save me.
Lord, help me to learn from past storms and trust You
in the future. Keep me safe.
Lord, be close to me in storms and keep me from
permanent harm. Guide me to still waters.

Are you walking the valley at night, not knowing where you are going? Are you afraid the next step will be your last? Remember, the Lord is with you. But do you really know it? Do you recognize His presence? Can you feel Him right behind you?

Lord, where are You now?

Some walk in the night—not in the darkness of sin but rather in simple ignorance. They don't know the Lord is with them. They have lost their bearings. They are like the two disciples on the road to Emmaus on that first Easter Sunday afternoon. The disciples were walking with the Lord, talking to the Lord and listening to the Lord, *but they didn't know it was the Lord* (see Luke 24:13-16). The two disciples had not wandered into sin; they were just blinded by preconceived ideas. The Lord was with them, but they didn't know it.

Maybe you are walking toward a storm without even realizing it. There is no great rebellion or sin in your life, so you don't think you are straying from the fold. You are just going your own way, doing your own thing. Then suddenly you realize that the dark night of trouble is upon you. Even then, the Lord is with you.

Lord, help me see Your presence in my life at all times.

An earthly shepherd can't know everything, and he may not realize it at first when one of his flock wanders off. But no one can wander from the heavenly Shepherd. He *does* know everything! He knows when you disobey Him and when you go off to feed yourself on the husks of this world. Do you realize that the

Lord goes with you when you sin? Nothing happens in your life that catches the Lord off guard.

Lord, I'm grateful that I can't wander away without Your knowing it.

If the Lord knows all things and is always with you, then why doesn't He stop you from wandering? Why doesn't God do something to keep you from sinning? That's a good question. Your answer is found in the essence of Christianity. Theologically, the answer is *human responsibility*. The heavenly Shepherd lets His sheep make some decisions because they are responsible for their walk with Him.

The Lord did not design us to act like stuffed animals—the kind that grandmothers bring as gifts for their grandchildren. While a stuffed sheep is a nice toy to keep a grandchild happy, it's not God's plan for you and me. We are not stuffed sheep. The Lord wants you to love Him, obey Him and worship Him. The Lord wants you to be an acting, thinking, responding person. Because the Lord wants something from you, He created you with the freedom of choice. You can choose—or refuse—to love Him.

So now you can give the Lord something that *He* wants. God has everything except your worship. The Father wants to hear you say "Thank You" and "I love You." The human response of fellowship can't come from a stuffed sheep; it comes only from the heart of one who is made in His image. It comes from one who has the ability to say yes or no.

Because the Lord made you like Him, you have freedom to choose—God lets you decide whether to remain near His camp or wander from Him. Do you see the picture? A sheep begins to wander from the Lord, and the Lord knows it. Usually, the sheep doesn't know what it's doing. A sheep chooses to feed himself on the chaff of this world, rather than eating in the green pasture provided by God—and the Shepherd knows His sheep is making a bad choice.

What does the Shepherd do when you begin to stray? First, He speaks to you through your conscience, saying, *Don't do it!* But you go there anyway. Next, the Shepherd speaks to you through His Word, the Bible. You know what is right because you heard the Word preached in church or sang the message of Scripture in

The Shepherd takes care of you, even when you don't see His hand working in your life.

hymns. But still you disobey. Sometimes the Shepherd speaks to you through the laws of government, and at other times He speaks through the natural consequences of your rebellion.

Lord, when I stray, come after me.

Some sheep ask, "Where was God when I strayed?" The 23rd Psalm has the answer: "You are with me." The heavenly Shepherd was with you from the moment you began to stray. He was your conscience telling you to stop. He spoke to you through the Bible and through your memory. He tried to stop you through circumstances. The Shepherd takes care of you in many ways, even when you don't see His hand working in your life.

Lord, I've strayed. Thank You for Your faithfulness in coming after me.

The heavenly Shepherd walks patiently with you through the dark valley, waiting for the occasion when you finally realize your sin . . . when you are sorry for your disobedience . . . when you turn back to Him . . . when you repent and seek His fellowship. When that moment of realization comes, cry out like a lost sheep. He will be there to help you.

The prodigal son demanded his share of the family inheritance and then squandered it on riotous pleasures and fairweather friends. When his money ran out, his friends left him and he ended up feeding pigs. When he was hungry, he had to eat pig food. Then, the Bible declares, "he came to himself" (Luke 15:17). The prodigal son was fed up with his life, so he cried out, "I will arise and go to my father" (Luke 15:18). Have you been there, done that? Have you come to yourself in the pig-pen? Are you willing to return to your heavenly Father? He awaits you with open arms.

Lord, search out any hidden sin in my heart that keeps me from You.

Why does the Lord go with His sheep when they wander away from His sheepfold? Because He wants to be there when they come to their senses. The eternal Shepherd is with you so He can receive you back to Himself. Then He will bring you out of the dark valley. Have you been lost in any dark valleys lately?

Your Turn to Pray
Lord, in the past I have wandered away from Your
presence and fallen into trouble. Thank You for
making me see my mistakes.
Lord, I'm grateful that You came seeking me when I strayed.
Thank You for Your presence in the dark nights.
Lord, it's good to be home with You and to enjoy Your presence.
Keep me close to Your side.
Lord, I promise I'll never leave You again. I want to be
near You. Don't let me wander.

CHAPTER ELEVEN

YOUR ROD AND YOUR STAFF, THEY COMFORT ME

The shepherd is not afraid of danger, because he knows the safest trail through the valley. The shepherd is courageous because he has a club—a rod—to drive away the enemy. The shepherd loves his sheep; and he is not reluctant to use his rod, nor is he fearful to attack an enemy. And because he knows how to use the rod, enemies keep their distance. He knows the ways of the predators.

Father, because You know the enemy, I will walk with You.

The shepherd also carries a staff to guide the sheep in the right paths and to rescue them when they fall into cracks and crevasses.

Lord, teach me to be cautious about the temptation of sin and help me to aggressively overcome its dangers.

> Yea, though I walk through the valley of the shadow of death, I will fear no evil; for You are with me; Your rod and Your staff, they comfort me (Psalm 23:4).

People usually think of the rod and staff as being the same thing, but actually they are two different instruments carried by the shepherd. Before the days of pistols and rifles, the shepherds had to make their own weapons. Many shepherds didn't have an ax or a knife to fight off their predators, so they used the best means available. The shepherd's rod was usually a thick, heavy stick—sometimes with a heavy knot on one end, carved from a root or tree joint—that was used to club an enemy. The shepherd could send a wolf running with a good, hard *whack!*

Using the best tools available, shepherds became skillful in defending their sheep. Some shepherds preferred to carry a short heavy club, so that in a close battle they could smash a predator's head. Other shepherds liked a longer club to keep the predators at a distance. Many shepherds kept a shorter club fastened to their belts, always ready to defend the sheep.

Lord, I thank You for Your weapons that can protect me.

The shepherd also had a staff, usually as tall as his head—sometimes taller—with a hook, or crook, at one end. The staff was made when a stick was tender, supple and green; it was bent into a crook and allowed to harden. The staff was used for directing the sheep. When sheep didn't follow their shepherd, he would reach out with the staff to direct straying sheep back into the fold.

The shepherd often used the staff as a walking stick to steady himself when climbing over large rocks or when small gravel shifted under his feet. The crook at the end could be used for rescuing a lamb that had slipped off the path or fallen into a creek. The shepherd tenderly placed the crook under the lamb and lifted it back to safety.

Lord, because I will need to be rescued many times in my life, keep coming after me.

Are you a sheep that wanders from the shepherd into the dark valley? When the enemy appears, what instrument do you use to defend yourself? Do you use your skillful arguments? Your money? Your position? Your education? So often we depend on our own tools and not on those of the Shepherd. The Shepherd's rod is available to defend us, but the club is wielded by the Shepherd, not the sheep.

Not once in God's Word does it mention a sheep carrying a club to defend itself. Nor do they have a staff for rescuing another sheep. Sheep have to depend entirely upon their shepherd for direction and safety. How about you? Are you depending entirely upon the Shepherd for your direction and safety?

Lord, help me learn the folly of self-defense. Teach me the security of Your defense.

Your Turn to Pray
Lord, I rely on myself too much, and I think I can fight my
battles alone. Help me see how You protect me.
Lord, I am fearful of the enemy, and I don't want to fight.
I only get hurt. Protect me from the enemy.
Lord, I have lost many battles because I have fought in my
selfish strength. I yield to Your protection. Help me see it.
Lord, I want to be victorious over the enemy.
Come fight for me and deliver me.

In this world, we live with more stress and pressure than ever before. There seem to be more temptations around every corner waiting to tear us down, and we often have more bad days in life than good days. We seem to be constantly climbing over problems—mountains that block us from moving forward in God's plan for our lives. Isn't it good news that the Shepherd will comfort you both on the path and when you get to green pastures?

Lord, I know trouble is coming. Help me get ready for it.

Isn't "comfort" a strange word to be used in this psalm? Isn't comfort something you expect from a bowl of chicken soup or a warm bed? How can you be comforted when you're walking through a dangerous valley—or when you're climbing, crawling and running through the obstacle course of life? The problem with the word "comfort" in Psalm 23 is that in our modern language it suggests the wrong thing—it suggests resting. Technically, the word "comfort" here can be translated "help." You could read this promise, "Your rod and Your staff, they *help* me."

If a wolf attacks, you don't want to try hiding under the covers of a comfortable bed; the wolf will find you and devour you.

Instead, you want the help of a fearless shepherd wielding a lethal club. Once the shepherd swings his club and the wolf runs away, then you are comforted. So in that sense, the club is a comfort to you. So when you think of the word "comfort," think of the results the sheep experiences when the shepherd's club protects it from the wolf.

THINK CAUSE AND EFFECT TO UNDERSTAND COMFORT

Cause	Effect
Thy rod helps me.	I feel comforted.
Thy staff directs me.	I feel assured.

Jesus called the Holy Spirit the Comforter, much like the club and staff are a means of comfort. Jesus promised, "I will pray the Father, and He shall give you another Comforter . . . the Spirit of truth" (John 14:16,17, *KJV*). The Comforter is not like a blanket on a bed, nor is the Comforter a person who comes to soothe you when you are emotionally upset. "Comforter" comes from the Greek word *parakletos*, which means "helper." The Holy Spirit helps you live the Christian life. He helps you through difficult times, and you are comforted. This is why He is called the Comforter.

When sin sneaks up to deceive you, the Holy Spirit is there to use His club to protect you from evil. How does the Holy Spirit keep believers on track? He uses negative influence, *conviction*, to warn you of sin and keep you pure and holy.

But the Holy Spirit also employs a positive influence, *guidance*, to lead believers into the truth. His guidance is similar to the shepherd's staff that gives direction to the sheep.

So how does Jesus the Shepherd comfort you? By the ministry of the Holy Spirit who comes to warn you when you stray into sin, and by the Spirit's ministry of directing you into the will of God.

Your Turn to Pray

*Lord, I've lost battles and been defeated many times.
Teach me to trust You and not myself, and give me victory
now and in the future.
Lord, I'm afraid of sin and the enemy. Teach me
to always trust in You.
Lord, I don't ever want to fight again. I'm weary
and afraid. Prepare me mentally for the next battle,
and give me courage and strength.
Lord, I sometimes feel I can't hold out and the enemy
looks fierce. Come and fight for me. Defeat my enemy
and give me peace.*

We all go through dark valleys; everyone has troubles. But you don't have to be afraid of the shadows in the valley because of the promise, "You are with me." The Shepherd is not only with you; He carries a big stick.

When you are walking near to the Shepherd, look up every once in a while at that big menacing club dangling from His belt. It will make you feel secure. You don't have to be afraid of it. The Lord loves His sheep and would never use a club on them. The club is for the enemy.

Lord, show me the club when I'm most fearful.

Some sheep in the fields don't follow close to the shepherd because they're afraid of him. Perhaps they're afraid because he yelled at them when they strayed. Has the Lord ever yelled at you? Sometimes you are like the sheep, straying too close to the edge of the cliff, in danger of toppling over. For your own safety, the Shepherd yells, "Come back!" But you misunderstood His intent and thought the Lord was angry with you because He shouted at you.

Lord, help me always understand when You shout at me.

Once there was a little lamb that continued straying into the thicket . . . near the edge of the cliff . . . into deep water . . . and near the wolf's lair. Finally, out of frustration, the shepherd broke the little lamb's leg. Then he tenderly bandaged it with a splint. The little lamb could no longer wander away from the shepherd; it had to stay nearby for food and drink. When the flock was led to another pasture for food, the shepherd carried the hobbled sheep. When they reached their destination, the shepherd caressed that little lamb more than the others. Why? Because the little lamb needed more love after it had been disciplined by the shepherd. Has God had to discipline you? Has the Shepherd broken your leg or shouted at you to bring you back to Him?

Lord, help me obey so You don't have to shout at me.

The Shepherd has a club to protect you, but He would rather not use it unless He has to. No right-thinking shepherd ever picks a fight with a wolf, bear or lion. The shepherd could be wounded in a battle, and some of his sheep could be hurt or maimed. There seems to be a lot of sin around you, and Satan

Be sure the Lord is your Shepherd, so when the final battle comes, you will be on the Shepherd's side.

seems to be having his day. Have you ever thought that maybe the Lord hasn't picked His final fight yet with Satan because He is protecting His sheep on the earth? When it comes to the final days and the Lord pours out His tribulation on the earth, Satan will lash out at God's people in retaliation. That final day of judgment is coming, and God will be ready for the confrontation. Just make sure the Lord is your Shepherd, so when that day finally comes, you will be on the Shepherd's side.

Jesus tells about the many enemies of His sheep. Sometimes Satan poses as an "angel of light" (2 Corinthians 11:14) and comes in among the sheep to destroy them. The enemy is like a thief sneaking into your house at night to steal your property (see John 10:10). Sometimes false teachers sneak into churches to steal sheep from the Lord. False teachers are like muggers who sneak up behind you to club you and steal your money. They deny the essence of Christianity, robbing the Bible of its supernatural nature. They deny the miracles and the power and necessity of the Lord's death and resurrection.

The hireling is also an enemy of the sheep. He watches sheep just for the money; so when the wolf comes, the hireling runs away, because he is more interested in self-protection than in guarding the sheep (see John 10:11-13).

The wolf is Satan who comes to "steal, kill and destroy" (John 10:10). The enemy will steal sheep because he wants their allegiance, often to help him steal other sheep. But Satan is the natural enemy of the sheep. He will kill you for no other purpose than to destroy your life.

WHO ARE THE ENEMIES OF THE SHEEP?

The stranger (John 10:5)—unprepared ministers
The thief (John 10:10)—false religious teachers
The hireling (John 10:12)—uncommitted ministers
The wolf (John 10:12)—Satan

If you are a sheep that belongs to the Lord, there will always be danger. You need the Lord nearby. There will always be someone trying to destroy you, so you need the Shepherd's club to protect you.

The rod is an important instrument for a shepherd. Moses was a shepherd in the Sinai Desert for 40 years. When God called him to service, Moses hesitated. God told him to throw his rod on the ground, and it became a serpent. This was a miraculous demonstration of God's authority in Moses' life (see Exodus 4:1-5). Later, to demonstrate God's power to Pharaoh, Moses' brother Aaron threw his rod to the ground and it, too, became a snake. The sorcerers of Egypt duplicated the feat with a pseudomiracle, a magic trick, but God demonstrated His greater power as the serpent of Aaron swallowed up the serpents of the magicians (see Exodus 7:8-12).

For Jewish shepherds, the rod was not just a weapon; it also contained the family genealogy. Just as some American families write their genealogy in the family Bible, so the head of each Jewish family carved his genealogy on his rod (see Numbers 17:2). When a father was about to die, he would pass his rod on to his sons, and it was kept in the family to remind them of their lineage. Some believe that when Moses wrote the genealogy of the various families of Israel, he was copying the names from the family rods.

One of the basic teachings of Psalm 23 is that the Shepherd has a way to teach us. When a Jewish son misbehaved, he was disciplined with the family rod. The son was not beaten just to inflict pain, but rather, the rod reminded the disobedient son of family expectations, family tradition and family authority. "He who spares his rod hates his son, but he who loves him disciplines him promptly" (Proverbs 13:24). Has God had to discipline you lately?

Lord, keep me in close relationship to the Shepherd.

Your Turn to Pray
Lord, forgive me for when I used my weapons against the
enemy. I failed by not trusting You and the weapons
You use to defeat the enemy.

Lord, I know You have weapons to defeat our enemy.
Your weapons are much more powerful than mine. Teach me
to trust Your weapons and Your power to defeat our enemies.
Lord, when the night gets dark and the enemy scares me,
remind me to look up to see Your rod and staff.

The staff is the most recognizable symbol of shepherding; we have all seen pictures of a shepherd holding a staff with its crook at the upper end. When you walk through the valley of dark shadows, glance up every once in a while to see the staff of your Shepherd high in the air. Watch for the Shepherd's crook in front of you. When you see it leading the way, you have nothing to fear.

Lord, help me to keep my eyes on You.

Sometimes three or four shepherds will bring their sheep together for a period of time. At night when the sheep go into the sheepfold for protection, one of the shepherds will sleep across the door of the sheepfold to protect the animals throughout the night. The next morning, as the sheep leave to go out to pasture, a shepherd will take his staff to separate his sheep from others, pulling out those that belong to him.

The shepherd will also use his staff to pull a "dumb" sheep in the right direction or push away a sheep that doesn't belong to him. Again, the shepherd doesn't want to hurt the sheep; he only wants to make sure his sheep stay close to him. Has the Lord been pulling on you lately? Maybe it's because you are not staying close to Him.

Lord, help me yield to Your direction when You pull me to come to Yourself.

A shepherd lifts up his staff over the sheep to bless them. When Joshua led the Israelites into battle against the Amalekites, Moses went up onto a hill to watch the battle and to pray for victory. Moses said, "I will stand on the top of the hill with the rod of God in my hand" (Exodus 17:9). When Moses held up the rod in his hand, Israel prevailed in the battle; but when Moses lowered his staff, Amalek beat back the forces of Joshua. So two companions held up Moses' arms until the victory was realized, because the uplifted staff was symbolic of God's blessing.

Lord, raise Your staff over me.

There is little comfort in this world. Most of us don't think to give comfort to others, because we are busy seeking it for ourselves. This is a lonely world with very little love for other people. When you are lonely, scared and looking for help, you need to know that the Shepherd has tools to comfort and protect you in your hour of need.

When everything goes right in your life, you don't seem to need the Shepherd. You satisfy your appetite in green pastures and drink from pools of still water. You sense no danger, no anxiety and no fear. You think you don't need the Shepherd anymore, and you soon forget about Him. But when the first sign of danger arises, you desperately look around for Him in the dark of night. Isn't it true that some of the greatest lessons you have learned were in the darkest time of night?

Lord, help me learn so I don't need to go through the darkness.

When you pass through the waters, I will be with you; and through the rivers, they shall not overflow you. When you walk through the fire, you shall not be burned, nor shall the flame scorch you (Isaiah 43:2).

The Shepherd never promised to shield us from sorrow. But when sorrows come, He will go through the troubles with you. The Shepherd did not promise that you would not die or get sick; but when these things come, He will accompany you through the long, dark night. God is true to His Word, so depend on His presence.

Lord, thank You for Your promise and Your presence.

CHAPTER TWELVE

YOU PREPARE A TABLE BEFORE ME IN THE PRESENCE OF MY ENEMIES

In Psalm 23, the sheep do not eat until they have been led through a threatening valley of dark shadows. Exiting danger, the sheep enter a lush green pasture that provides more than enough food. This is a picture of a table of food spread before them. Now the enemies of the sheep can't attack them; they can only watch from a distance as the sheep graze peacefully in a bountiful pasture.

Thank You, Lord, for the joy of anticipation.

> You prepare a table full of food to feed me in the presence of my enemies (Psalm 23:5, author's paraphrase).

Notice where your table full of food is located—not in a secluded castle in a faraway land, but in the presence of your enemies. Usually when you come through a scary valley—a dangerous situation—you come out the other side running. Maybe you are not literally running, but on the inside your heart is racing. When running from danger, you are not thinking about a meal. All you are thinking about is escaping the predator that is dogging your footsteps. You are obsessed with the need to escape to some protected spot. You want to climb a tree that death shadows can't climb; you want to hide behind a protective wall that death shadows can't penetrate.

Thank You, Lord, for Your guidance through my dark days.

Being scared to death takes your mind off your hunger—frightened people do not think about food. But the Shepherd thinks differently. He not only wants His sheep to feel safe, He wants to provide a place for them to eat until they are satisfied. A table full of food makes them feel confident and victorious. Because the Lord is your Shepherd, He will lead you from a threatening situation to where you will enjoy an abundant meal.

Lord, thank You for making me feel secure.

Has God fixed a good hot meal for you lately? It is there for the eating, so why don't you sit down and make yourself at home? Come taste the appetizer of love and feel God's presence. The table is filled with bowls of salvation, so everyone can eat, no matter what they have done. There is a platter full of hope and excitement for the future. And there are enjoyable desserts of inner happiness. Come drink and you will never thirst again. If you hunger and thirst after righteousness, God will more than satisfy your needs and your heart's deepest desires.

Just as you eat to satisfy your hunger, you will find inner joy at His table. Just as you drink to quench your thirst, you will find complete fulfillment at His table. Just as a good meal makes you healthy, you will find strength and spiritual growth at His table.

But there's one thing better than food at His banquet: the intimate fellowship you share with someone you love as you eat a meal with Him. You will commune with your Lord at the banquet table: "My beloved is mine and I am his" (Song of Songs 2:16). At the Shepherd's banquet table, you will get close to Him, learn from Him and become like Him.

Lord, forgive me for not always feeding on the bread of life.

Psalm 78 describes Israel's desperate condition from wandering 40 years in the wilderness. The nation had disobeyed God by refusing to enter into the Promised Land, so to punish their unbelief God relegated His people to four decades of wandering in the wilderness. During their journey, Israel asked in unbelief,

"Can God prepare a table in the wilderness?" (Psalm 78:19).

Is that a question you ask? When I'm being chased by a death shadow, too scared to eat, can God feed me? Can He spread a table in the wilderness? Can I ever be secure again?

What is His answer?

You prepare a table before me in the presence of my enemies . . . my cup runs over (Psalm 23:5).

As you run from danger, God does not give you a quick squirt of water from a plastic bottle like you're a boxer between rounds. You are not like the marathon runner swigging water as he frantically dashes toward the finish line. The next time you are running scared, remember what's waiting for you outside the valley: a full table and an overflowing cup.

Lord, I hear You saying, "Come, sit down and eat."

Think of an antelope being chased by a lion—it doesn't have time to drink and eat. When we are in danger, most of us tend to panic when we feel that time is running out. In desperation we cry, "I must do something!" Our hearts pound . . . we sweat . . . we gasp big gulps of air. We keep saying, "I've got to get away!" Stop and let the Lord feed you and give you a gigantic drink of refreshing water. Relax. You don't need to "eat and run." Take your time for a spiritual feast, because the Lord has spread a table in the presence of your enemies and your cup overflows.

Your Turn to Pray

Lord, my problems are getting me down and defeating me.
Help me look beyond my problems to see the banquet table
when I get out of this valley.
Lord, thank You for being with me in my problems and for
delivering me from my unique death shadow.

Lord, I'm scared of the enemy but You've promised to be
with me in the darkness. Help me feel Your presence and
deliver me from the evil one.
Lord, You've promised me "good times" after the valley.
Give me strength to hang on in the darkness.
Lord, thank You that there's a banquet table for me
in the future. I claim it by faith.

You need to tell yourself that it's okay to pause and breathe. God has invited you to a great feast of spiritual food, but do you know how to find His restaurant? The meal is called Communion, where you get to know God intimately. Nothing else in life satisfies like knowing God; and no food will taste as good as obeying His commandments: "Oh, taste and see that the LORD is good; blessed is the man who trusts in Him!" (Psalm 34:8).

When you pick out a restaurant, what are you looking for? Good food, good service and a nice atmosphere. The ambiance, or setting, is just as important as the food, because good food can't be enjoyed in filthy surroundings. Nor can you enjoy a meal when you're surrounded by people yelling or fighting. To enjoy a meal takes more than good food in your mouth; it involves the entire experience. So why does the Shepherd feed us in the presence of our enemies? Isn't that a strange setting in which to throw a feast?

Why would God feed His sheep in the presence of our enemies? Perhaps it's a victory banquet, and God is telling our enemies that He can protect His sheep from them. Perhaps it's the other way around. Maybe God is telling *us* that He has conquered all our enemies, so we will trust Him the next time we are in a dark valley. The Shepherd knows His sheep. He knows we will stray again into the dark valley, and He knows there will be dark shadows pursuing us in the future.

Lord, deliver me constantly from the evil one.

Once the shepherd gets his sheep through the valley, there's food waiting on the other side. The shepherd knows where the green pastures are located, and he leads his sheep there. The shepherd wants the sheep to feed when they first get there; that's the reason he brought them through the dangerous valley. He doesn't take sheep through the valley just to experience danger or to demonstrate that he can deliver them from danger. He takes them through danger to get to the pastures on the other side.

When the Lord is your Shepherd, you have nothing to fear—plus you get a good meal to eat.

As the shepherd leads his sheep through the dangerous valley, predators may have followed. Once they are safe in green pastures the sheep enjoy the tender grass, but in the distance the predators watch. Nevertheless, the sheep don't have to worry. Why? Because the shepherd is there to keep the enemy away. His club and staff will protect the sheep. You must remember that as long as you are in good relationship with your Shepherd, you have nothing to fear—plus you get a good meal to eat.

When the psalmist uses the word "presence," what does he mean? Obviously, when two people meet, they are in each other's presence. But the enemy of the sheep is not sitting next to them at the banquet table. Sheep and predator are not even in the same pasture. Or to put it in today's terminology, they're not even on the same block. When you eat in the presence of your enemies, that means they can see you—but only from a distance. Perhaps the wolf is on a cliff or the bear is lurking in some dark woods. They are in the presence of the sheep, or in their sight line, but sheep and predator are worlds apart because of the shepherd. Is the Shepherd protecting you?

Lord, I feel safe in the Shepherd's care.

David uses the words "my enemies" (Psalm 23:5), which refer not to just any enemies but rather *personal* enemies. Perhaps the enemies were those who had a vendetta against David's life—i.e., Saul or Absalom—or murderers set to kill David. Do you have enemies? Do you have someone who particularly hates you? If you have enemies, God will give you a feast so they can look on to see His protection.

Remember, the feast is nothing if you don't sit at the table, eat and enjoy yourself. This is how the Shepherd shows the predators lurking among the rocks that He takes care of His own. Do you complain when God delivers you? Stop it! Do you take credit for getting yourself through dark valleys? Don't! Why do you take credit for the Shepherd's protection and victory? Be a good testimony to your enemies; eat God's food and enjoy His protection. It's the best way to get back at your enemies. It's God's way.

The word "enemies" has an unusual ring to it. David doesn't tell us we will eat in the presence of evil persons, although there is much evil in the world. David doesn't mean we will eat in the presence of robbers. After all, robbers merely want to steal from you; they probably don't hold a grudge against you. David chose the word "enemies" to show that there is hatred or animosity between the predator and the sheep. Remember, there are people in this world who hate God's sheep. They hate sheep just because they're sheep. And they particularly hate you, because you are the Lord's sheep.

Lord, I belong to You. Protect me.

Even though the enemy is separated from you as you feed in the Lord's pasture, never miscalculate your enemy's nature or underestimate his craftiness. The devil is a roaring lion seeking to devour you, and lions roar when they are hungry. The enemy wants to devour you not just because he hates you but also because he hasn't had a meal in quite a while. The enemy is furious that you're eating while he's hungry. Nothing would give your enemy more satisfaction than to tear you limb from limb. When you see your enemy lurking in the shadows, lean close to the Shepherd. Every time you feel a little threatened, lean even closer.

Lord, I feel secure next to You.

Your Turn to Pray

Lord, I've been wounded by my enemy, and defeat hurts.
I come to You for healing.
Lord, I have a particular enemy who wants to destroy me.
I pray for my victory and his defeat.
Lord, my enemy scared me because I kept my eyes on the
problem instead of on You. Forgive me for my faithlessness
and help me overcome my problem.
Lord, I know there is security by Your side, but I tend
to stray. Keep me close to You.
Lord, thank You for Your banquet. Even though I don't
deserve it, may I always feed in Your presence.

Don't let the enemy deceive you. Even when he's not chasing you or attacking you, he's still your enemy. Max Lucado tells the story of an old man attempting to climb the highest mountain. During his climb, the old man met a snake who asked, "Will you take me with you? I've never been to the top."

The old man said, "No. You'll bite me."

The snake promised, "I'll not bite you." So the old man put the snake inside his shirt and continued climbing.

When he finally reached the top, the old man looked around. It was the fulfillment of one of his life's dreams. He remembered the snake and took it out from under his shirt.

Suddenly the snake struck the old man, sinking his fangs into the old man's flesh. As the venom filled the man's veins, he cried out, "But you promised you wouldn't bite me!"

The snake laughed, answering, "You knew what I was when you picked me up."

Many young people pick up a drug because it promises not to bite, but they become addicted. Have you been victimized by Satan's lies? Remember that your enemy may attack you by deceiving you. He's the father of lies, but you are safe resting next to the Shepherd.

Lord, protect me even when I don't know I need You.

You probably live your life as a series of threatening valleys and enjoyable banquet tables. Like other believers, you are not exempt from dark days. As Job observed, "Man who is born of woman is of few days and full of trouble" (Job 14:1). Because the Shepherd loves you, He won't let you spend your whole life in the middle of storms. Sun will shine upon you some of the time. You may go through a dark valley, but there will be a sunny pasture waiting for you on the other side of your trouble.

Lord, help me make it through.

Why do some sheep have more valley experiences than others? Only the Shepherd knows. Why do some sheep have more banquet days than others? The Lord has a different purpose for each life. What's His purpose for you? No one can answer but the Shepherd, so get close to Him.

Perhaps you are constantly threatened by death shadows and the night terrifies you because you've never learned to walk alongside the Shepherd. You are in more danger than others because you walk too close to the edge of the precipice.

Lord, keep me close to You.

When you have finished eating from the Lord's table, do not jump up and start running again. Do not look around nervously for the death shadow or listen for the voice of the enemy. The Shepherd has said, "Surely goodness and mercy will follow [you] all the days of [your] life" (Psalm 23:6). If you think the death shadow is still following you and you are still trying to escape, you are looking for the wrong thing.

Learn to look to God, and when you find Him you'll realize the sound behind you is not the enemy. It's the sound of God's goodness and mercy following you according to His promise. And He will send goodness and mercy to follow you all the days of your life. He will protect you and take you to live with Him in heaven when this life is over.

Now, come to His table. Your cup is full, the food is warm and ready, and it's time to sit down and eat. The Lord is there, for He has said, "I will be with you."

CHAPTER THIRTEEN
YOU ANOINT MY HEAD WITH OIL

You needed oil today. Why? Because you came through a death valley where the thorns scratched your legs. You fell in a ravine and ripped your arm. When you came out of the valley, the Shepherd anointed your wounds. He poured oil on them to cleanse them and prevent infection and disease. The oil was soothing. It relieved irritation and began the healing process.

Lord, cleanse me from any sin or imperfection that would infect me.

The Shepherd remembers that at special banquets, certain honored guests have oil poured upon their heads in recognition of their attendance at the meal. It is an oil of acceptance and honor, and the one who is anointed with oil is given special recognition by all the other guests at the banquet.

Lord, thank You for Your unique anointing on my life. May I fulfill Your purposes for my life.

You prepare a table before me in the presence of my enemies; You anoint my head with oil (Psalm 23:5).

The first thing on the mind of sheep after they leave a dark, threatening valley is their appetite and thirst. After he has seen to those needs, the shepherd has another concern. He examines the wounds of his animals. He knows that if impurities are not washed away, a wound will get infected. He also knows that oil will speed the healing process. So while the sheep are eating in the pasture, the shepherd is busy cleansing their wounds with oil. Each wound is carefully washed. Now healing can begin.

Jehovah-Rophi, thank You for healing me.

Do you have any wounds that might fester? Have you received any dirty cuts from gossip? Have you been roughed up by the opposition? Maybe you have some gashes or burn marks because someone told lies about you. What are you going to do about these problems? Let the Shepherd pour out His oil of cleansing to rid you of any dirty sin or damaging wounds. Forgive those who have lied against you and those who have gossiped about you. Pray for those who have abused you.

Sometimes when you pray good for your enemy, you are praying "coals of fire on his head" (Romans 12:20). But don't pray for judgment on your enemies; pray instead for God to bless them. Sometimes the only way for God to bless them is to deal with their sin. But judgment is not your concern. Get everything between you and God straight, then let God deal with things between Him and them. Ultimately, we want our enemies to turn and follow the Shepherd as we follow Him—even those who have sinned against us the most. When you pray in the Holy Spirit, His oil will cleanse you from impure attitudes that could otherwise destroy your life if you were to allow them to fester.

Lord, cleanse my attitude.

But the shepherd pours on oil for more than just cleansing; he knows oil feels good. Left unattended, the sheep's wounds will burn, itch and sting. Sometimes a wound throbs with unceasing pain. Have you ever had a headache you couldn't get rid of? Have you ever worked so hard around the house that every muscle in your body ached? What about emotional problems? Have you ever had a heartache that wouldn't go away? Have problems ever invaded your dreams so you could no longer sleep? What you need is oil from the Shepherd. You need the oil of the Holy Spirit to soothe your pain.

Lord, thank You for pouring the oil of the Holy Spirit on my life.

Do you need some oil today? Make sure you are resting near the Shepherd so He can reach out to pour oil into your wounds. There is no advantage to sitting by yourself, away from the flock and away from the Shepherd. Don't hurt just for the sake of hurting—that's neurotic. Lift your head, look around to find the Shepherd, then cozy up close to Him so He can anoint your wounds with oil.

Lord, here I come!

Your Turn to Pray

Lord, I hurt. I feel terrible. I want to feel better and
I need Your help. Come anoint me with oil.
Lord, there is some dirt in my wounds; I confess to You that it
was my sin that put it there. I'm responsible for my impurities.
Forgive me of my sin, cleanse me and make me pure.
Lord, I need Your presence because I hurt and feel far
away from You. Pour the oil of the Holy Spirit on my life.

As I mentioned earlier, in Bible times honored guests were anointed with oil. They were given a special place at the table and special portions of food that others did not receive. Do you feel like you have been eating at the foot of the Lord's table? Maybe you feel like you have been eating in the kitchen! But the Shepherd has a special place for you, and He has a special plate of food. Come, there is a chair reserved for you. Eat from the best china and use the silver utensils. You are an honored guest, because you are one of His sheep.

Mmm, this food is good, Lord. Thank You for accepting me.

Some scholars think an aging David wrote the 23rd Psalm while fleeing from his son, Absalom, who had rebelled against his father and taken over the kingdom. Let's travel back for a moment to steal a glimpse at what David might have experienced during this difficult time in his life.

As David writes about the Lord as his Shepherd, his thoughts take him back to when, as a mere 16-year-old boy, he was anointed as the future king of Israel. It was near the Kidron Valley in Bethlehem where the prophet Samuel had come to the house of Jesse, David's father, under the direction of God. There in the presence of his father and brothers, Samuel poured oil over David's head and anointed him into the office of king (see 1 Samuel 16:1-13).

Now, many years later, David has only a handful of loyal followers, as he is forced to abandon his throne and the security of Jerusalem. The elderly David has been forced to flee down the same Kidron Valley toward the plains of Jordan. Imagine it: As David turns to look back up at Jerusalem, he knows he is leaving the city that stands for the central authority of his kingdom. All the symbols of his power have been stripped from him—there's no throne, no crown, no scepter, no walls of Jerusalem to protect him. David has lost all his outward authority, yet still—*still!*—he can write, "The Lord is my shepherd; I shall not want."

God had placed David into the office of king, but now his son Absalom is trying to kill him. Absalom has taken over the office with crude force. With tears in his eyes, David remembers, "You anoint my head with oil."

In biblical days oil was a symbol of kingly authority, because oil was special to God. In Israel at that time, candidates for prophet, priest and king were inducted into these divine offices by anointing with oil; prophet, priest and king all had oil poured on their heads.

What does memory do for David? He remembers that God took the initiative to anoint him. Memory can do the same for you. Remember that it was your heavenly Shepherd who came looking for you when you strayed from His fold. Remember that it is the Lord who has always loved you and cared for you. He brought you back to Himself—not to punish you but to give you food to eat and water to drink. In spite of everything you have done, the Lord anoints your head with oil.

Lord, I don't know why You anoint me with oil, but thank You.

Do you understand the full meaning of oil upon the head? The angel told Mary that her son Jesus would sit upon the throne of David—her Son would be the *Anointed One.* That phrase, "Anointed One," is "Messiah" in the Hebrew language and "Christ" in the Greek language. When we use the word "Christ," we are actually saying "the Anointed One." When we say "Jesus Christ," we are saying, "Jesus the Anointed One."

We have already said that prophet, priest and king were the threefold anointed offices in Israel. But what does that mean to you and your walk with the Shepherd? The Lord anoints you with oil to give you a special position in relationship to Him. First of all, because you belong to Jesus, you are "in Christ" (1 Corinthians 1:30). You are in the Messiah, the Anointed One. Jesus told His disciples about their special position: "You in Me, and I in You" (John 14:20) describes the intimacy all believers would have with God's Son. So when you read about the Lord anointing you with oil, remember that you are in Christ and that He is in your heart.

How close are you to God the Father? You are as close as His Son, for you are in His Son, and He is in you: "Christ lives in me" (Galatians 2:20).

Lord, anoint me with the oil of Your presence.

There is another meaning associated with oil. In Scripture, oil is a symbol of the Holy Spirit. When we are anointed with oil, it is a picture of the Holy Spirit coming into our lives. When you first accepted Christ as your Savior, the Holy Spirit entered your soul, bringing with Him eternal life. When you face special tasks of service, you can be filled with the Holy Spirit to do the job for God. The New Testament mentions that the disciples were filled with the Holy Spirit when they ministered for the Lord (see Acts 2:4; 4:8,31). Then there are other times when you just want the fullness of the Holy Spirit in your life. You want His anointing. Have you had the Holy Spirit poured out on you lately?

Lord, I want the anointing.

When the shepherd anoints his sheep with oil, he doesn't anoint all his sheep. He can't anoint those that are straying, nor can he anoint those that are busy eating and drinking. If you are out of arm's reach of the Shepherd, how can He anoint you? If you are not in the pasture, there is no way He can anoint you. The key to being anointed by the Shepherd is relationship. You must be close to Him. Are you within arm's reach of the Lord?

If you are out of arm's reach of the Shepherd, how can He anoint you?

Lord, I'm coming over by You. Will You anoint me?

To receive the anointing of the Holy Spirit you must recognize that there are steps—things you must do to get it.

You must want it. Do you honestly want the Holy Spirit in your life?

Get within arm's length of the Shepherd. You need to be close enough for His loving arm to reach out and pour the oil of the Holy Spirit on you. Isn't this a good time to move closer?

Seek the Holy Spirit's oil. You have to know where the spout is located and then stand under the flow. Seeking God has always been a key to revival—both personal and group revival. Seeking God means spending time in prayer and meditation. It means worshiping God and enjoying fellowship with Him. When you see the oil pouring out somewhere else, go there to stand under the spout. When you see others with oil on their heads, go talk with them, pray with them and find out how they obtained the oil. Maybe they will help you position yourself for the outpouring of His oil.

Open up your life to the Holy Spirit. You can't open your life until you pay attention to the Shepherd. This means yielding, surrendering, dedicating or consecrating yourself. You become passive and let God take over the rule of your life.

Ask for it. "You do not have because you do not ask" (James 4:2).

Receive it by faith. What do I mean by faith reception? Think of pouring syrup from a jar. (This comparison is used because syrup's consistency is similar to that of a heavy oil.) When you tip the jar of syrup it takes a few seconds before the syrup actually starts dripping from the spout onto your waffles. When you have asked for the fullness of the Holy Spirit, you may not get it immediately. It's not because the Shepherd can't give it immediately. Maybe He is not ready to give it because you're not ready to receive it. Maybe you have hidden sin in your life that needs uncovering and cleansing. Maybe you are not yet close enough to Him. Maybe the Shepherd is looking for faith on your part to believe that you will receive. So when you tip the jar and the oil doesn't come out immediately, keep praying, keep believing—you need patience. Wait for the anointing of the Holy Spirit, and it will come if you wait long enough.

Keep your cup under the spout. Don't go running all over the place looking for other oils that run out faster. You can't come to church once or try God for one day or pray once for an answer. The Lord is looking for true believers—those who mean business. If you didn't get your cup filled, don't go looking elsewhere for fun and pleasure. That's not the answer.

Finally, you must act on the anointing when it comes. When you get the Holy Spirit, use the anointing for the reason that He was poured out upon you: to receive God's blessings and share them with others. Rejoice in the Lord, worship God, then serve other people.

Your Turn to Pray

Lord, I've run all over the place looking for fun and pleasure,
but I haven't found deep satisfaction; I know it is found in You.
I commit myself to seeking You as hard as I sought a good time
in the world. I will seek You with all my heart.

Lord, I'm empty and powerless—my life is running on empty.
I don't have spiritual ability to live for You or serve You.
Pour oil on me today.
Lord, I want the Holy Spirit in my life. I'm waiting for Him
to anoint me with oil. Fill me now!

CHAPTER FOURTEEN

My Cup Runs Over

It's been a long, hot trip through the barren desert. Your Shepherd is up ahead, guiding you and the flock to lush green pastures. You begin to realize how thirsty you are. Then a familiar, welcome scent reaches your nostrils: water. The thought of water makes you walk faster, more confidently. Then you see it—a pasture and a cool, still pond of crystal-clear water. The pasture is like a table spread before you with all the enjoyable food you can eat. The pool of pure water looks like a cup—your favorite cup—that's running over with your favorite drink. The pool is large and deep, but you can see clear to the bottom. You know you could never drink it all. It's all you can drink—and more.

Lord, thank You for good water to drink when I'm thirsty. Thank You for providing even more than I can drink.

Thou preparest a table before me in the presence of mine enemies . . . my cup runneth over (Psalm 23:5, *KJV*).

Consider the phrase "my cup." When you come to the Lord's table, you don't see a strange cup, a new cup or a beautiful cup. While these may be nice, when you're thirsty, you want to drink out of *your* cup. Have you ever noticed how many people have a favorite cup for drinking their coffee? Many people keep a favorite coffee cup at work so they don't have to drink from a paper or styrofoam cup.

Thank You, Lord, for letting me drink from my cup.

You know it's not your parents' cup—you can't live on your parents' religion. They may be Christians and, if so, the Shepherd has filled their cups on many occasions. But in God's house, everyone has his or her own cup. So don't try to drink out of your parents' cup. Get your cup from off the shelf and hold it under the flow until it is filled. Then you can claim the promise, "My cup runneth over."

The psalmist didn't say, "My cup ran over," describing the past blessings of God. Some people always talk about what God did for them in the past. Some have never washed out the foam from yesterday's blessing. Each day they go to the shelf and inspect their cup to see if the foam from a previous blessing is still there. They may even run a finger around the inside of the cup to get any lingering taste. Find the spout that's pouring out today's blessing and get your cup refilled. Then you can praise God and say, "My cup is running over *now!*"

Lord, let it flow.

Some say, "My cup *will* run over." Right now their life is empty, and they are thirsty. If you pressed these people, they would have to say, "My cup is empty." But as soon as they confessed their thirst, they would optimistically predict, "My cup will overflow someday." Do you live in the future? Do you plan to have the power of God someday? Do you plan to study the Bible all day or go to a retreat center where you will fast and pray for a day or even several days? Don't rob yourself of today's blessing by living in hope of a future that may never get here. My friend John Maxwell says, "Life is a journey, not a destination." You can have a full cup today.

Lord, fill my cup now.

Still other people think they have many cups. They pray optimistically, "Lord, fill up all my cups." But that's not what the psalmist says. He describes *one* cup: "My cup runneth over." Some people have a "church cup," and they want it filled on Sunday. They have another called the "job cup," which they want filled on payday. The student wants his "school cup" filled on exam day. And young people want their "happiness cup" filled on date night. There are almost too many to mention—sports cups, family cups, hobby cups, etc. Many have a cup hidden away in a closet that is locked. It's a lust cup or addiction cup.

The problem is you really only have one cup, and it's *you*. All that you think and do touches every part of your life and then ricochets back to touch the original part. Your one cup is your whole life. God doesn't just fill one area of your life; He takes complete control or nothing at all. He fills all—or nothing at all.

When you say "My cup runneth over," you're saying God influences all of your life with His presence.

Your Turn to Pray

*Lord, You've filled my cup continually, but I've been
too blind to see Your blessing. I've been too rebellious to drink
what You have poured. Forgive me for wasted opportunities
and give me one more big drink.
Lord, I have only one cup, and it's not very big. I have a
powerful thirst. I want to drink deeply from Your blessings.
Lord, teach me the theology of the cup, so I will know
when to drink, how much to drink and what to do
when I'm filled up.
Lord, teach me the obligation of now. I have only
one cup—I have only today for sure. Fill my cup now,
and I will drink immediately.*

What do you think the psalmist means when he says "runneth over"? If this happens on most of our tables, mother runs to wipe up the spill. Most people don't want their cups running over; they don't want spills. If you are the legalistic kind, you are more concerned about what's spilling out of the cup than with what is being poured into it!

Perhaps the phrase "runneth over" is just a picture of abundance, and the Shepherd doesn't intend for us to spill or lose anything. Perhaps the words "runneth over" are a metaphor to communicate fullness and sufficiency. Whatever it means, is your life running over with the Shepherd's blessing?

The phrase "runneth over" could refer to the source of the blessing. Perhaps it means God has so many blessings that He can pour them out on us and still have more. Remember, God doesn't have a warehouse of blessings that will run empty sometime in the future. The Shepherd doesn't store up His blessings in any case. He is the Blesser, He is unlimited and His blessings are unlimited. He pours them out continuously. If God had a pitcher of blessings, it would never run empty. Don't worry about getting left out—God will never run out of blessings.

When Jesus was thirsty, sitting on the edge of the well in Samaria, a woman arrived at the well with a bucket. Jesus said, "Give me a drink" (John 4:7). The woman at the well had been married five times and was now living with a man who was not her husband. She was probably suspicious of men and of Jesus in particular. After all, Jesus was a Jew and she was a Samaritan.

"How is it that You, being a Jew, ask a drink from me, a Samaritan woman?" she asked.

Jesus answered, "If you knew the gift of God, and who it is who says to you, 'Give Me a drink,' you would have asked Him, and He would have given you living water" (John 4:9,10).

Perhaps she thought Jesus meant continuous running water, like the faucets in our modern kitchens. She might have envisioned an artesian well where water continually flows. The woman wanted her bucket filled so she would never have to come to the well again. If you are the Shepherd's sheep, you never have to worry about thirst again. He will fill your cup to overflowing forever. Would you like that?

What does it mean that your cup will always be filled? God will always pour out a blessing. That doesn't mean you won't have financial problems, health problems or family problems; but when troubles come, you will have spiritual blessings from an overflowing cup.

The blessings are always flowing, because the tap is always open. But some are thirsty and choking to death for lack of water. Why? Because they refuse to bring their cup to the Shepherd to let Him fill it. If you are thirsty today, don't blame God or your friends. Drink is available, but you have to grab the cup, lift it to your lips and take a big gulp. Go ahead, do it.

Lord, Your water makes me feel good. I sure need it.

What are you going to do about all that liquid in your cup? It's so full that it's running over. Think about the One who fills your cup. God has been generous with you in the past, just as He

Go ahead. Grab your cup, lift it to your lips and take a big gulp!

is pouring plenty of blessings into your cup at the present time. Isn't it time you think about others? Since God has filled your cup to overflowing, you should share with others. The blessing of God is not something you can stash away or hide; you have to give it away as you receive it.

Lord, help me not to look in the bottom of my cup as I drink. Help me to lift my eyes toward others.

The Lord gives you more than you can drink—more than enough. He gives "exceedingly abundantly above all that we ask or think" (Ephesians 3:20).

Do you have a cup? Look inside to see what blessing is there from God. Is it full? Half empty? If your cup is not full, will you let the Shepherd fill it for you? It is easy to get a full cup, because the Shepherd has more than enough to fill yours and the cup of every other sheep that comes to Him. Not only does the Shepherd have many blessings for you, but He also wants to fill your cup today.

So how do you get your cup filled? First, you have to *want* a full cup. This means you must get honest with yourself and God.

You need to confess, "I'm thirsty, and I want a drink of water." The Bible says, "Open your mouth wide, and I will fill it" (Psalm 81:10). If you want a drink of water, the Shepherd will give it to you.

The second step involves loving God. Do you love the Lord who shepherds You? Jesus said, "If anyone loves Me, he will keep My word; and My Father will love him, and We will come to him and make Our home with him" (John 14:23, author's paraphrase). Receive that promise. If you love Jesus, both He and the Father will make their home in your heart. That's the same as filling your cup. You are the cup, and Jesus fills you with Himself. That's abundant blessing!

The third step is to ask God to fill your life. If you are empty, it's because you have never asked God to fill your life. "You do not have because you do not ask" (James 4:2). Why don't you pray right now for God to fill your cup?

Lord, fill me.

There's a fourth step to having an overflowing cup: You must *receive* what the Shepherd offers. When someone offers you a cup of coffee or hot chocolate, what do you do? You reach out and take it! You can't drink from the cup until you receive it. If you fight the entrance of God into your life, then you can't be filled.

Why would you fight God? Is it because you know He wants you to be holy? To drink from the cup, you will have to rid yourself of sin. He wants to fill your mind, so you will have to change your vocabulary and allow Him to purify your thought life. The Shepherd wants to fill your life totally, so you will have to restructure your calendar. You will have to adjust your business and family life according to His principles.

Don't compromise: You may only want to give the Shepherd half your life, but He doesn't deal with half a cup. In the restaurant you can ask for half a cup of coffee, but the Shepherd will not pour your cup half full. And the Shepherd won't compromise with a dirty cup. He will not pour pure water into a dirty vessel. Why should His pure water be contaminated by your dirty cup?

But then, the Shepherd never asks His sheep to "do the dishes." He knows sheep can't wash dishes! If sheep have dirty cups, they can't clean them up by themselves. So the task of cleaning the cup belongs to the Shepherd.

What must you do to get clean? You must ask Him to cleanse your cup. All you have to do is be willing to get rid of sin. Determine that you want a clean cup and ask the Shepherd to wash out the dirt. "If we confess our sins, He is faithful and just to forgive us our sins and to cleanse us from all unrighteousness" (1 John 1:9).

Lord, come wash my dishes.

Now that you are ready to have your cup filled and overflowing, I hope you have not missed the point that your overflowing cup is your whole life. When He fills your cup, He fills every part of your life. Some people want God to fill their mouths but not their hearts. So they go to church and say the right things, but they hold evil thoughts in their hearts. Other people want God to fill their hands for work in church, but their eyes still desire sin. Still others want God to fill their feet to do good deeds, but they are not willing to have God cleanse their attitudes. If you don't offer the total cup to God—your whole life—He can't fill it for you. Where is your cup? Why don't you hold it up to God with both hands?

Some people want God to fill their cup to the brim, but not a *smidgen* over. These are believers who fulfill every obligation at church but don't go the extra mile. They only do what is required of them. They give exactly a tithe of their income but not a penny more. But you can't bargain with God. You must give Him everything, so He will fill your life to overflowing. He will pour so much blessing into your life that it will spill over!

Have you ever spilled any blessings into someone else's cup? When your cup runneth over, splash it around and let some others get wet!

Your Turn to Pray
*Lord, stretch my expectation because I've settled
for a small sip of blessing from the cup in the past. Give me
faith to want more, and give me ability to do more.
Lord, I love to drink when You fill the cup. It never
empties, because You keep it full. May I never
become satisfied with little swallows.
Lord, You've filled my cup with the water of
eternal life, and I will live forever with You.
May I always drink deeply of eternity.
Lord, help me to live generously. Just as You've
been generous in filling my cup, I want to
give out more than I take in.*

CHAPTER FIFTEEN

SURELY GOODNESS AND MERCY SHALL FOLLOW ME ALL THE DAYS OF MY LIFE

Can you feel spring in the air? Your spirit is refreshed by the gentle breeze that blows over the hills and the palette of clouds that cut the heat, making it a perfect day. Your Shepherd is nearby, and there is enough food to eat and water to drink—you don't have a worry in this world.

You never plan to leave the Shepherd, nor do you intend to stray away from the flock. Sometimes you get so busy feeding yourself, however, that you just wander away. But when you begin to stray, goodness and mercy pursue you and bring you back into the fold.

Lord, thank You for good things that keep me near You and for Your mercy that pursues me when I stray.

Surely goodness and mercy shall follow me all the days of my life (Psalm 23:6).

You left the valley of death where death shadows were pursuing you—you could feel them biting at your heels. You thought you were going to be destroyed, but God brought you out of the valley to a lush green pasture. And what do you see? A table loaded with meats, fruits and desserts. You see the Shepherd pouring so much into your cup that it is running over. You have all you can eat and drink, but as you get up to leave, where do you plan to go? Don't go back into the valley where the death shadows lurk! Rather, stay close to the Shepherd so He can lead you to the next destination.

Lord, thank You for good days when I feel great. May I trust You in good days, as I do in the dark, scary valley.

As you begin following the Shepherd, something is nipping at your heels. You are scared momentarily, because you think death and destruction are on your trail. But in fact it is the Lord's sheepdogs, Goodness and Mercy. They are right behind you to make sure you stay in the flock. Why are you worrying? God's goodness is giving you wonderful things to keep you in the flock, and God's mercy is overlooking your failures. These two sheepdogs will pursue you—not just today but for the rest of your life. Don't worry, you have the Shepherd up front guiding you and his two sheepdogs following you to make sure you keep up with the flock.

Lord, why am I worrying when You are taking care of me?

The first sheepdog is Goodness. The shepherd sees one of his sheep wander after some foreign grass just a little way from the flock, so he sends his sheepdog to chase the wandering sheep back to the flock. The shepherd doesn't throw a rock or stick at the sheep to hurt it. He doesn't want to hurt his sheep, nor does he want anything else to hurt it. The shepherd doesn't say, "If the sheep falls into the ravine, that will teach it a lesson."

The Shepherd does *good* things for his sheep—even when they stray too far away. "The goodness of God leads you to repentance" (Romans 2:4). What good thing has the Shepherd done for you lately? Are you in good health? Do you have shelter against the rain? Have you eaten today? Do you have a family who loves you? Look at all the good things you have. A good God wants to do good things for you.

Lord, give me an eye to appreciate all the good things You do for me.

The second sheepdog pursuing you is Mercy. The Shepherd has mercy because "God...is rich in mercy" (Ephesians 2:4). When you are rich with something, you have an abundant supply to share with others—and God has an abundant supply of mercy. Unlike the shepherd who has a few things tucked into a bag to help him with his duties, God has more than just a pocketful of mercy. The very nature of God is mercy. God has more than just a warehouse full of mercy. God is a factory, a mercy maker, and He will never run out of it.

As a matter of fact, when God began listing His qualities to describe who He is, He listed mercy first. Moses asked to see the glory of God, so the Lord descended in a cloud to Mt. Sinai to answer him, proclaiming, "The LORD God, merciful and gracious, longsuffering, and abounding in goodness and truth"

The Shepherd loves you and chases after you with good things.

(Exodus 34:6). First, God says He is merciful, but He adds that He has abundant goodness. That is where the two sheepdogs get their names. And when they are playfully running after you, they don't have a separate agenda from the Shepherd. They do the same things the Shepherd does for His sheep. The Shepherd has taught His sheepdogs well: They do good things for the sheep, and they show mercy to His charges.

There are two sides to mercy, just as there are two sides to a door. The first side of the door is God's side: Mercy reveals God's character. He loves you and chases after you with good things. If you have sinned against Him, the Shepherd has something good for you: He has *forgiveness* in His Shepherd's bag. If you have turned your back on God, the Lord has *restoration* in His satchel to bring you back into the fold. If you deserve punishment for your rebellion, the Lord has *grace* in His bag, not a whip with which to beat you.

Grace is God's way of giving you the exact opposite of what you deserve, rather than punishing you for being a stray sheep. In mercy the Shepherd hugs you close to Himself and rejoices over you. What do you and I prescribe when a child misbehaves or runs away? Punishment. What do we get when we run from God and then come back repentant? Restoration and fellowship! That's mercy.

Lord, have mercy on me!

But there is a second side to the door of mercy—our side. You felt threatened in the dark valley with death shadows chasing you, but what do you feel now? *Relief!* When you are relieved, your pain, distress and fears are removed. When the Shepherd shows mercy to you, your anxiety melts and you experience relief.

When you are sick and in pain, the Shepherd binds up your wounds, pouring in healing oil to relieve your suffering. That's mercy. When you are in financial debt and cannot pay your bills, the Shepherd gives you a table full of food and a house in which to live. That's mercy. When you've messed up a project at work and you think you're going to be fired, but you work through the project with your boss, you feel relieved. That's mercy. Even more, you feel relieved when you don't get fired. That's mercy. When you say that God has mercy, you are describing the relief He gives you from the threat of death shadows. That's mercy. You feel good when the Shepherd brings you out of the storm. That's relief. That's mercy.

Paul understood mercy when he said, "Christ Jesus came into the world to save sinners, of whom I am chief . . . for this reason I obtained mercy" (1 Timothy 1:15,16). Before his conversion, Paul hated Christ. He persecuted the Church and was responsible for the death of Stephen, one of Christianity's most promising young leaders. What a terrible blow to the Church! Did God punish Paul for blasphemy and murder? No! God forgave his sins so he could say, "I have obtained mercy."

What do you deserve from God? Have you denied Him? Have you strayed from His fold? Have you cursed with His name or broken His commandments? Do you need mercy?

Yes, Lord, give it to me!

David demonstrated the meaning of mercy for us. After he became king, he called a servant to ask, "Is there not still someone of the house of Saul, to whom I may show the kindness of God?" (2 Samuel 9:3). This seemed a strange request, because Saul had driven David out of Jerusalem and into the wilderness. For 13 years Saul had pursued David, intending to kill him. David had lost his home, family, security and place of service. David could have had revenge in his mind with an eye toward eliminating any heirs of Saul who would have been a threat to David's throne. But David didn't want to get even; he understood the mercy of God and he wanted to show it to others.

David found there was one heir left—a grandson of Saul's named Mephibosheth. When the boy was quite young, an accident had left him lame for life. David's servants brought the crippled Mephibosheth to the king's table, and David said to him, "Do not fear, for I will surely show you kindness for Jonathan your father's sake, and will restore to you all the land of Saul your grandfather; and you shall eat bread at my table continually" (2 Samuel 9:7).

David later proclaimed, "As for Mephibosheth . . . he shall eat at my table like one of the king's sons" (2 Samuel 9:11). Now that's mercy! One who deserved to be punished for what his grandfather had done is rescued and brought to the king's table like one of the king's own sons. How did Mephibosheth feel? Relieved, joyful, accepted and chosen. How do you feel when the Shepherd brings you to His table and gives you all you can eat?

Lord, it feels good to eat at Your table.

Your Turn to Pray
*Lord, I'm glad You don't send punishment after me
when I sin. Thank You that Your sheepdogs Goodness
and Mercy are pursuing me.
Lord, I worship You for being good. I magnify You for being
merciful. Help me always to see the good things You do for me.
Lord, thank You for Your mercy that pardons the evil
things I do. I will live a victorious life because of this
unbeatable combination.*

You feel so good that you want to pet the two sheepdogs. But you can't, because they are on the move, dashing back and forth to bring stray sheep back into the fold. When all the sheep are safely in the fold and lying down in green grass, the sheepdogs lie quietly next to the shepherd. Now you can pet them. If you do, they'll nuzzle up to your foot as if to say, "Pay attention to us." That's the sheepdogs' way of telling you not to forget God's goodness and mercy. Both should be a constant presence in your life's journey, giving you encouragement and peace.

Have you ever noticed how few things in life are "for sure"? Someone once said that nothing is certain except death and taxes. However, the psalmist uses the word "surely." The Shepherd is telling you that some things *are* certain: "Surely goodness and mercy shall follow." No matter where you go, they will follow you, sticking to you like glue. You can't shake the Shepherd's sheepdogs—they'll stick with you forever.

The psalmist doesn't say they *might* follow. A conditional promise could become an unfulfilled promise if we were to stray from the Shepherd. If the psalmist had said "might follow," it would have meant, "If we follow the Lord, *then* His sheepdogs will follow us." But that is not the message of Psalm 23. This is a psalm of relationship. Surely goodness and mercy shall follow you, even when you stray into the valley of the shadow of death. The Lord is with you, and goodness and mercy will still chase you.

Why goodness and mercy together? Because goodness is what your mother gave you when you were hungry. She prepared hot biscuits, cold iced tea—and there was even a dessert after the meal. The kitchen was warm, your bed was clean and because your mother was good, she gave you good things. Likewise, the Shepherd does good things for you because He is good.

But there was another side to your mother: She was merciful. When you scraped your knee, she applied medicine to the wound and wiped away your tears. She didn't scold you for being careless. When you failed at sports or any other endeavor, your mother listened to you. The Shepherd is like that. He is good to the sheep that follow close to Him, but He is also merciful to those who stray into the dark valley. He brings you back safely to the fold, all the while rejoicing over you.

Lord, I praise You for being both good and merciful.

When the psalmist says "goodness and mercy shall follow me," he is painting a picture of being closely followed or pursued. It is a picture of someone chasing another to catch up with them. You have seen a dog chasing a car, and you've seen movies about a sheriff's posse chasing the bad guys in a Western. Do you realize that God has His two sheepdogs chasing you? They're not trying to bite you! They want to do good things for you and show you God's mercy.

God's sheepdogs are following you, but maybe you don't realize it. Perhaps you don't see the Lord working in your life. You go around being terrorized by evil, when the Bible says, "Greater is he that is in you, than he that is in the world" (1 John 4:4, *KJV*). You are continually obsessed with the evil death shadow that you think is chasing you. You need to remember that you belong to the Shepherd, and He takes care of His own.

How far will the sheepdogs pursue you? Maybe you think Goodness and Mercy pursue you only when you go to church or do something good for God. You think God is not near on a stormy Monday morning or worse, when your car is stuck in a snowbank. You think that God has deserted you, if you think about Him at all. But remember that the Lord is with you in the valley, and He sends Goodness and Mercy to chase after you when you slide backwards. On good days and bad, Goodness and Mercy are following you—just turn around and see.

Lord, open my eyes.

Your Turn to Pray

Lord, there are so few things in life that I can count on.
Yet You promise me that I can count on Your goodness and mercy. Help me to see it daily in my life.
Lord, You have been good to me. You have given me more than I deserve. Thank You for Your bountiful goodness.
Lord, You have forgiven me every time I've strayed from Your side. Thank You for Your mercy to forgive me and restore me every time I drift away.
Lord, forgive me when I look around to see if the devil is catching up to me. Give me faith to look around to see Your sheepdogs, Goodness and Mercy, following me.

CHAPTER SIXTEEN

AND I WILL DWELL IN THE HOUSE OF THE LORD FOREVER

Although David conceived of Psalm 23 when he was only a boy shepherding sheep for his father, he wrote it while fleeing from Jerusalem as an elderly man. As he escaped down the Kidron Valley, David looked back over his shoulder toward the fortified walls that he had built surrounding Mount Zion. Maybe David thought he was getting his last look at the city of David.

He had done everything he wanted to do except build a temple. When David began gathering materials to construct a magnificent temple to Jehovah, God stopped him, saying, "Your son Solomon will build My temple" (see 1 Chronicles 28:6). As David took his last look at Jerusalem he prayed, "May I dwell in God's house forever."

Lord, that's my prayer, too. I want to live with You forever in Your home.

> Surely goodness and mercy shall follow me all the days of my life; and I will dwell in the house of the LORD forever (Psalm 23:6).

The capstone of David's rebuilding of Jerusalem was to be the Temple. It was to be the crowning pinnacle of his life's ministry. But now David is escaping beyond the Jordan with nothing but a dream in his heart: to live in God's house. David doesn't weep over his lost palace, his servants or the adoration of the fickle crowd—the same crowd that was now praising his son, shouting,

"Long live king Absalom" (see 2 Samuel 16:16). David has a passionate hope—to live in God's house—that will keep him alive as he sleeps this night on the ground.

As long as a man has hope, he's not dead, nor is he dying. A man with a vision of doing something for God is more alive than his enemies who do not recognize God.

Lord, I have a dream. Help me to realize it.

To understand the vast ramifications of this final verse of Psalm 23, you must remember where shepherds live. They don't live in a house. They sleep in a tent, usually a cold tent. Many times their only source of heat is a fire—if they have one—at the tent's door. They sleep on hard, unforgiving ground, not in a soft, warm bed. Would you like to live the rest of your life in a tent?

Thank You, Lord, for a roof over my head, a floor under my feet and a bed to sleep in.

Sometimes the shepherd has to sleep under the open sky, his roof the stars. His only protection from the cold is the tunic that also protects him from pouring rain and beating sun. Nor does he have a change of clothes. A shepherd sleeps outdoors with no walls to keep out snakes, scorpions and other venomous creatures. So what is the shepherd's ultimate dream in life? "I will dwell in the house of the LORD forever."

Lord, I want more than a house to live in. I want to live with You.

God has promised David that his son Solomon will build the Temple and that Solomon will be the next king. David should be happy at the thought of his son carrying on the family name. But David isn't thinking about Solomon or his other son Absalom, who has stolen the kingdom. David still has a dream: "I will dwell in the house of the LORD forever."

The word "I" has deep meaning for David. *He* will dwell in God's home; *he* will fellowship with God. He wants it for himself—not for his sons, not for other shepherds, not for Israel in general. This is personal for David.

What do you want from God for yourself—not for your family or your Sunday School class? Relationship is always personal, and you can have a personal relationship with God. You can dwell with Him forever.

Lord, I must know You; I must live in Your presence.

The word "dwell" here does not mean to sleep. While we do sleep in a house or apartment, the word "dwell" means more. Some seem to think "I will dwell" means "I rent space in God's house; it's mine for a short while." When David pens this remarkable psalm, he is not dreaming of a temporary stay in God's house. He wants to settle down in it and make it his permanent residence.

Lord, I want to dwell in Your presence forever, never to leave it.

A shepherd camps where the night finds him. Sometimes he camps on a windswept mountain, at other times in a secluded valley. The camp is usually an overnight situation—a temporary place. Think of Israel's wanderings in the wilderness for 40 years—no roots, no familiar surroundings and no permanence. If you were camping as the Israelites camped, you couldn't get

You need to rest with God in His house.

used to the water supply. You couldn't get comfortable with anything. You would live in a constant state of change, over and over picking up and moving from one place to the next. Change would be your bed, your coat, your seat and your table.

Lord, I thank You for some degree of permanence in my life.

The word "dwell" suggests a place of rest. Where do you rest best? Usually we rest most soundly in our own bed at home. While camping is exciting and we relax during a camping vacation, have you ever said, "I need some rest to get over my vacation"? Why is that? Probably because you worked or played too hard on your vacation, and now you need to go home to rest. The word "dwell" suggests you are going to sleep in your home and you're going to get some rest. Are you tired from too much stress? Maybe you're tired from too much play. What you need is to rest with God in His house.

The shepherd knows when his sheep need rest, so he makes them lie down in green pastures. When does God give you rest? The Lord gives you the night so you can rest from each day's heat and work. The Lord gives you rest each Sunday, so you can recover from the pressures of the week. Heaven is called a place of rest (see Hebrews 4:1-10). The Lord makes a place for us, heaven, where we will one day rest from the trials we have now on Earth.

Lord, I need rest. Help me take advantage of the opportunities that are mine.

Your Turn to Pray
Lord, I need rest; I'm weary and life is difficult. Renew my strength for today and help me serve You afresh tomorrow.
Lord, I feel like I'm just camping out here on Earth.
While I manage to get some physical rest,
I need "soul rest," too. Renew me.
Lord, I look forward to good sleep tonight and working hard tomorrow. May I get strength from my sleep and new purpose from my rest.

"Dwell" is a wonderful word to a shepherd. It means more than a place to stay awhile or a place to sleep for the night. The word "dwell" suggests to "abide in a home" or to "settle down with your family" or to "feel secure." Because most shepherds had no home to go to at night, they probably dreamed of a warm, quiet place where they could rest each evening. What is your dream?

David's passion is to live in the house of the Lord. Remember that as a boy, David tended sheep under the open sky. As a fugitive he was pursued by Saul for 13 years in the Judean wilderness. That's a long time to sleep on the ground. Yet, even before Absalom drove David out of Jerusalem, he had a passion for God's home: "For in the time of trouble He shall hide me in His pavilion; in the secret place of His tabernacle He shall hide me" (Psalm 27:5). When David is once again pursued by enemies, what is the one thing he wants most?

> One thing I have desired of the LORD, that will I seek:
> That I may dwell in the house of the LORD all the days of
> my life, to behold the beauty of the LORD, and to inquire
> in His temple (Psalm 27:4).

David had a passion for the house of God that Solomon would eventually build. This would be a permanent replacement for the moveable and temporary Tabernacle, or Tent of Meeting, which was a tent designed to be the meeting place between God and His people. Let's examine this Tabernacle more carefully. Scholars are not sure where the Tabernacle was located during the time of David's youth. The Tent of Meeting originally housed the Ark of the Covenant in Shiloh (see Joshua 18:1). The Philistines later overran the nation of Israel in battle and took the Ark of the Covenant, placing it in a heathen temple among some of their own pagan idols. But God afflicted the Philistines with painful sicknesses, so they sent the Ark back to Israel (see 1 Samuel 5).

David's first attempt to return the Ark of the Covenant to Jerusalem was a miserable failure. He and his men tried to move the Ark on a wagon—contrary to God's directions. When the wagon lurched, God struck dead a man who touched the Ark (see 1 Chronicles 13:10). David was determined to do it right the next time, so he probably consulted the Scriptures. He ordered that the Ark of the Covenant be carried on the shoulders of the Levites, and continual sacrifices were made as the Ark was brought to Jerusalem. A great choir assembled at Jerusalem to greet the procession by singing the praises of God. Trumpeters were poised on the city walls to announce the coming of the Ark. There at the front was David, dancing mightily before the Lord. When all the people saw the procession of the Ark coming toward Jerusalem, they praised God (see 1 Chronicles 15:28).

But when David brought the Ark into Jerusalem, the Tabernacle itself—or what was left of it following the Philistine raid—was not in Jerusalem but, instead, was in Gibeon, a few miles away (see 1 Chronicles 16:39). So David pitched another tent on Mount Zion in Jerusalem specifically to house the Ark.

Many scholars think the separate tent David set up was his own private place of worship. The Bible says:

> Then King David went in and sat before the LORD; and he said: "Who am I, O Lord GOD? And what is my house, that You have brought me this far?" (2 Samuel 7:18).

When David sat before the Lord, he was sitting before the Ark of the Covenant, before the presence of God, who "dwelt" above the mercy seat between the cherubim on the Ark (see Numbers 7:89; 1 Samuel 4:4).

According to the Law of Moses, only the Levitical priests were allowed to enter the Holy of Holies where the Ark of the Covenant was kept. David was king, but he was not a Levitical priest. If it is true that David had a private tent which housed the Ark, David actually circumvented the Levitical law in order to be closer to the presence of the Lord!

Lord, let me follow You and dwell in Your presence, no matter the cost.

David understood that the presence of the Lord dwelt with the Ark, so he wanted the Ark near his house to receive the blessing of God on his home and life. At night, David wanted to see the people praising the Lord in the Tabernacle on Mount Zion: "Bless ye the LORD, all ye servants of the LORD, which by night stand in the house of the LORD" (Psalm 134:1, *KJV*). As David walked about his palace, he could look out over Mount Zion where the Ark of the Covenant was being kept in his personal tent. He saw people standing there praising God with their hands, blessing the Lord.

Lift up your hands in the sanctuary, and bless the LORD (Psalm 134:2).

The LORD that made heaven and earth bless thee out of Zion (Psalm 134:3, *KJV*).

David had a passion to live in the presence of the Lord; intimacy with God was his constant dream. David wanted to dwell forever in the house of the Lord, wherever that was. David constantly worshiped the Lord from his heart and blessed the Lord at all times. Do you have the passion of David to dwell in God's house and enjoy His presence? The good news for us is that we do not have to travel to Jerusalem or any other specific location to dwell in His presence. He meets His sheep where they live!

Lord, I love You. I want to dwell in Your presence to worship You.

When David said "I will dwell," he was making a *faith promise*. David knew God had blessed him and that the Lord was his Shepherd. David had such a strong relationship with the Lord that he had confidence he would one day return to the holy city to live with God.

Notice David didn't say, "I *want* to dwell." There are many things in life that you want but don't get. You may want a new car, a bigger house or the latest electronic gadget. You crave or desire something, not knowing if you will get it. When David said "I will dwell," he was making a statement in bold faith that

God would one day return him to Jerusalem and to the house of God. He knew he would live with God forever.

Lord, I know You will take me to heaven.

But there's another important meaning to the phrase "I will dwell." It is a statement of commitment. David was making a promise to return to God's house. This is something he had to do. When David said, "I will dwell," he was committing his wealth, his armed men, even his own life, to do whatever it would take to return to Jerusalem and the house of God. His son Absalom had run him out of his house and out of Jerusalem, away from the Ark and the presence of God. But when David said, "I will dwell," he made a promise to return and worship the Lord on Mount Zion.

Like David, we can conclude by saying, "I will dwell in the house of the Lord forever." This statement is the perfect ending to the most beloved passage of Scripture. Like David, we can be assured that through all of life's valleys and green pastures, our eternal home awaits—and we will dwell there forever with our Shepherd.

Epilogue

Now that you have finished reading and praying Psalm 23, what's next? Why don't you make the lessons you've observed in this book a part of your daily walk with God?

First, cultivate a faithful attitude of walking with your Shepherd every minute of every day, for the rest of your life. It's really quite simple. He's with you all the time, so talk with Him often.

Second, apply the principles of praying Psalm 23 to other portions of Scripture. Just talk to God as you read Scripture, asking Him to make the truths in His Word real in your life. Talk to God about the Scriptures as you read them. Then go a step further: Turn the words of Scripture into prayer. Talk to God using the words of the Bible.

Third, pray Psalm 23 on a regular basis. All of Christianity is in Psalm 23, as all of the oak tree is in the acorn; therefore, praying Psalm 23 means you are praying about every aspect of your faith. If you can only pray once a day, I suggest you pray Psalm 23.

Praying the 23rd Psalm

Because You are my Shepherd,
I commit my needs to You.
Provide green pastures for me to lie in,
Lead me beside still waters,
Restore my soul when I'm empty,
And lead me in right paths for Your name's sake.
Be with me in danger when I walk
Through the valley of the shadow of death.
Deliver me from evil
And protect me with Your rod and staff.
Prepare a table to feed me,
So my enemies can see Your provision.

Anoint me with the oil of Your healing.
Let me drink from the full cup of Your provision.
Surely goodness and mercy will always follow me,
And I will live with You forever.

For more information about other resources
by Elmer Towns, please write:

Elmer L. Towns
1971 University Boulevard
Lynchburg, VA 24502
etowns@elmertowns.com

Or visit the Elmer Towns Online Library at:
www.elmertowns.com

Put Your Prayer into Action

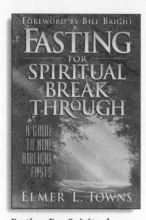
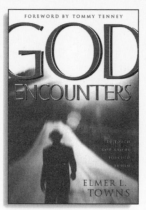

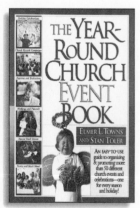
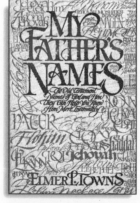

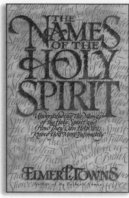

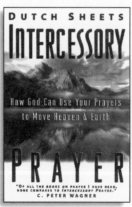